SCREAMING THROUGH THE SILENCE

Screaming through the Silence

Memories, Truths and a Hope Towards Understanding

Mary Ann Ricciardi

authorHOUSE®

AuthorHouse™
1663 Liberty Drive
Bloomington, IN 47403
www.authorhouse.com
Phone: 1-800-839-8640

First published by AuthorHouse   11/23/2011

ISBN: 978-1-4678-7154-9 (sc)
ISBN: 978-1-4678-7153-2 (ebk)

Library of Congress Control Number: 2011960737

Printed in the United States of America

Any people depicted in stock imagery provided by Thinkstock are models,
and such images are being used for illustrative purposes only.
Certain stock imagery © Thinkstock.

Front cover photograph courtesy of Shelly Reynolds
Chapter 1 photograph courtesy of Shelly Reynolds

"Now" clock (chapter 7) designed and created by Mary Burrows mbartstudios.com

Because of the dynamic nature of the Internet, any web addresses or links
contained in this book may have changed since publication and may no longer be
valid. The views expressed in this work are solely those of the author and do not
necessarily reflect the views of the publisher, and the publisher hereby disclaims
any responsibility for them.

For

Zayne Allen and Byrdie Gail
You are my heart as it dances and circles outside of my
body.

You are so worth the rant.

SCREAMING THROUGH THE SILENCE

CONTENTS

Author's Clarification

Not all perpetrators of intimate violence are male. Not all victims of intimate violence are female. But we do know that most perpetrators are male and most victims are female. Throughout this book, I will often refer to the perpetrator as "he" and the victim/survivor as "she." It is not my intention in any way to dismiss the painful trauma of the male victim/survivor or to ignore the criminal acts of the female perpetrator. It is merely my way of simplifying repetitive pronoun use.

PREFACE

I have often wondered if I would ever have what it takes to put pen to paper and scribble out what I know to be true about the life-changing pain and injustice of sexual violence. For years, I went along with the silence; it seemed safest for my soul. It seemed the most comfortable thing I could do for myself and those around me, those I loved and cared about. I know better now.

I now know our silence serves no good purpose. It deprives society of the understanding and knowledge that are necessary to care for victims and to deal with perpetrators appropriately. It delays the healing of victims and keeps them from transforming into healthy survivors.

These days, I am not at all concerned with society's discomfort regarding the issue of sexual violence. I care little about my own discomfort as I speak out. Let's face it, there is nothing comfortable about saying, "Yes, I was raped by four guys when I was eighteen, and I told no one." What I do care about are the countless precious spirits that have been and will be sexually abused and raped because we are too uncomfortable to speak up. We are too uncomfortable to pay attention and begin the conversation about what needs to be said and done.

I acknowledge we have made quite a bit of progress over the last forty years with the many crisis centers, women's shelters, and rape centers offering support and counsel to those in need. There are activists and advocates working globally to create positive change. And they are succeeding. But baby steps are excruciatingly slow when we know that the number of sexual assaults are so high and reports to law enforcement are so low. We continue to struggle with social silence. And I am impatient.

My background and career have always been in nursing and, as my husband would say, a "domestic goddess." I am not a psychologist, therapist, or educator. One might question my qualifications as I attempt to write this book. But what I do have is valuable experience, forty years' worth, which in my humble opinion matters. I have been the victim, the survivor, the silent one, the empowered one, and the advocate.

For the majority of my adult years, I stood in the shaded background and simply observed. That is all my silence would allow me to do. I watched, I listened, and I paid close attention to the world around me and wondered, *Why such tolerance?* I knew the silence did not feel right, but society was not talking and so neither would I. As I watched and listened, I hoped to catch a glimmer of outrage from a society that I believed to be good and just. But I barely saw it and I barely heard it. What became very obvious to me was a profound lack of understanding and an even greater discomfort regarding crimes of sexual assault and abuse, especially when it came to the lingering and long-term emotional aftermath a survivor is left to personally deal with. We have been slow in tending to the healing of these traumas. We have been slow to outrage. We have been slow in stopping the silence and encouraging understanding and awareness. I can only surmise it is in part due to the "vicious cycle" syndrome. Society cannot understand because victims do not tell; victims do not tell because society does not understand. But if society is expected to understand the complexities of sexual assault and abuse, voices must be heard. Stories must be told. Conversations must start. Silence on both sides of the fence must stop.

This book is short and sweet. Well, perhaps I should rephrase that. This book is short and not so sweet. It contains no scientific data to prove why, what, when, or where. Statistics will be limited because, quite frankly, statistics on the topic of sexual violence can be all over the place depending on which study you are viewing. I do not believe we need to rely on those numbers to tell us what we already know and have known for generations. Sexual assault is happening, and it is happening far too often. One undeserved, senseless rape is one too many.

I did not write this book with the purpose of telling my own story. Unfortunately, my own story is not at all unique. Believe me when I say, I wish it were. It gives me little pleasure to reveal a part of my life that has caused me such pain and loss and that, for a time, weakened my once strong spirit, leaving me psychologically and emotionally vulnerable. But I have written and shared, and along the way I have learned about the beauty of vulnerability and how it opens us up to be our genuine self, our more honest and truthful self.

It is precisely because my story is not unique that I am moved to write. With each new victim I sit beside and attempt to console, I remain acutely aware of the painful emotions that hide deep beneath the dull look in his or her eyes. I understand the struggle their spirits will be left to deal with as they go on their way. Perhaps for a day, a month, a year. Perhaps much longer.

My scenario may differ slightly from the scenario of another, but what is collectively shared in shameful numbers is the trauma to one's spirit and the long-term emotional aftermath that continue to quietly torment a survivor's world.

This shared trauma becomes evident as you read the words of the survivors who so willingly contributed to this book. Their words are their own. Their scenarios belong to them. The thoughts and feelings they chose to express came from a place of truth. They are individuals, yet in reading their words it becomes apparent that there is a common link to the emotional effects survivor after survivor identifies. Their emotions mesh together and seem to be shared by all.

I write to bring awareness. Yes, I know that some would refer to "awareness" as an overused word these days—overused, perhaps, but necessary. I am simply writing necessary truths in hopes of making some noise in my little corner of the world. My noise will be added to the noise others are already making, and, in turn, encourage many more to know that their voices and their stories matter. We can drown out the silence with our voices. Little by little, we can create the positive change necessary to fight sexual violence.

So I am compelled to write and rant. Yes, this will be my rant of sorts. I can offer to be a voice for those who have yet to find their own. And I know there are many. More importantly, my hope is that whoever picks up this book, and for whatever reason peruses its pages, might take away a thought or two that will bring him or her closer to understanding what needs to be understood about a darkness that weakens the spirit.

Whether you are hoping to find voices that match your own quiet thoughts, easing that sense of aloneness, or whether you are reading to genuinely gain a better understanding of the emotional aftermath of sexual violence or simply out of curiosity, I am grateful to you for choosing to pay attention to this serious and harmful social issue. We must not look away and tolerate the intolerable. Our silence must no longer be an option.

CHAPTER I

Silence

I knew as soon as they let me go that
I wasn't going to tell a soul.

*I*t is often difficult to make sense of the silence surrounding the issue of sexual violence, especially the silence of the victim. One would assume that a victim of a crime, any crime, would immediately report the incident to law enforcement or, at the very least, tell someone, anyone. But it does not always happen that way. Not with sexual assault and abuse, anyway. The number of sexual assault victims reporting to law enforcement hovers somewhere around 40 percent according to the US Department of Justice, Bureau of Justice Statistics (2008). An upsetting statistic, to say the least. Taking the path of silence, still today, is tempting to many victims of sexual assault which seems to be a very disturbing reflection of our society. Why should people who have been the victim of such a traumatic crime feel they are better off remaining silent?

But there are reasons, a long list of reasons, why victims stay silent. I hear them often as I sit beside victims, offering comfort and support soon after their assault. I listen to the painful stories they are willing to share with me, and I recognize the dullness in their eyes that tells me their spirit has been badly injured. I know they are wondering if anyone will really understand their story and if it is all better left unsaid. I know their painful journey is just beginning.

Some of the reasons for wanting to stay silent are clearly stated by the victim; some of their reasons I catch between the lines. There are victims who are not naive to society's attitudes toward rape victims and choose silence over the possibility of moral judgment by others. While this may be a temporary shield against additional and undeserved pain, I believe it will eventually suppress the healing process.

Regardless of their age at the time of the assault, many victims state they are fearful of telling their parents and loved ones. They are gravely troubled by the thought of upsetting parents and frequently choose to keep this information to themselves. They believe, often incorrectly, that they will be able to get through the experience on their own, sparing their loved ones from worry. They do not know their silence will most likely tug in the opposite direction of their healing.

Much of the reasoning behind the suppressed voice of victims can be linked to feelings of embarrassment, humiliation, and self-blame, but these emotions that a victim burdens herself with are the very emotions that only the offender should own. Never the victim. While I want to say that none of these reasons are good enough reasons to remain silent, I still honor and respect a victim's decision to not report. I understand.

My brain shuts down, unable to make sense of it all. What just happened? Why? I'm not comprehending, I'm denying . . . When they are done with me, they let me go. Just like that, they are letting me go. How do they know I will not tell? . . . I will drive myself home, and I will be okay. I repeat to myself over and over again, "You're okay; you're fine, you'll be just fine—keep driving. It's all over, you're okay." Shock keeps me sane for now. Denial protects my soul.

The detachment from who I once was has begun.

In his book *Men Who Rape: The Psychology of the Offender*, author Dr. A. Nicholas Groth states, "Rape is a topic that abounds with myths and misconceptions. It is a complicated, emotionally charged, and highly misunderstood subject" (1979, 1). His words continue to ring true today. If rape is too overwhelming for even the victim to make sense of, how can one expect society to grasp the devastating reality of the experience? It is an ongoing dilemma that desperately needs solutions. But we will get nowhere in the silence. Our silence as a society has helped contribute to the perpetuation of these crimes. Our silence, our discomfort, and our tolerance have allowed the perpetrator to move from victim to victim with little consequence. Speaking out will certainly help protect countless would-be victims from painful and undeserving trauma. This reasoning alone is powerful when reassuring a victim that her decision to report was the right thing to do—for herself and for the next possible victim. She may very well be preventing the perpetrator from harming yet another vulnerable spirit, and she is taking back the control of her own life that was briefly and cruelly stolen. There is no doubt that raising our voices as victims and as a society is absolutely necessary to bring about better understanding, knowledge, and awareness of these crimes.

My silence is my denial. To speak of it will only make it real. And it can't be real. My silence will erase all memory. My silence will let me be me again.

But it doesn't.

Stopping the silence means starting what I call the "squirm." You know, it is when something is so uncomfortable to deal with or talk about that we begin to squirm. It is a mental sort of squirm, an obvious reaction I often detect in casual conversation. Many of my fellow advocates and I have shared a chuckle or two about the reactions we get from people we encounter as we are asked about the kind of work we do. When our answer is "I work with victims of sexual assault," the majority of reactions are the same, which is, basically, no reaction. And the subject is quickly changed to anything other than the huge "pink elephant" that is standing in the midst of our society that no one thinks is going to bother them. I sense the "squirm."

This discomfort that causes us to squirm helps create a continuing silence that only benefits the perpetrator. But it does not have to be this way. We can stop this quiet discomfort by educating ourselves. These crimes are happening all around us and are often closer to our social circle than we think. Perhaps some of our discomfort and silence is fear based. Perhaps it is easier to deny that a member of our family or one of our friends could become a victim. We think these things only happen to other people so we need not be concerned. But fear and denial are not going to keep us safe or bring about solutions. Fear, denial, and silence are what perpetrators depend on. Acknowledging this and engaging in conversation can replace the discomfort with knowledge and understanding. And, as with any life issue, we know knowledge is power. If we can just get past that initial barrier of discomfort and break the silence, we can be on our way to making a positive difference in the fight against sexual violence.

I have a theory that I am quite sure has been explored before but one that I firmly believe deserves much more exploration and attention. It is our verbiage. When we talk about sexual assault, sexual violence, and child sex abuse, we are insinuating that these crimes have something to do with sex. They do not. The language we are using misdirects society to assume, incorrectly, that these crimes are results of behaviors of a sexual nature. The physical crime perhaps mimics the sex act, but that is as far as the similarity goes.

Most people enjoy sex; it is a pleasurable human experience. Normally, having sex with one's partner is a private matter, and it goes on behind closed doors to be enjoyed in whatever manner one wishes to enjoy it. Usually, it is no one else's business. So I am wondering if there is a small (or large) part of social thinking that considers sexual assault to be a rather unfortunate and upsetting experience, but wonders, how bad can it really be when most of us are having or eventually will have sex anyway? Especially when no gun, knife, or serious bruising is involved. Since having consensual sex is a most personal experience, perhaps there are still those who feel crimes of a sexual nature are meant to stay personal and private.

I believe these crimes have stayed personal and private for too long.

But, of course, it is complicated. The humiliation and degradation a victim suffers are understandably reasons to desire privacy after an assault. The very intimate way one's body has been violated causes untold embarrassment. Even when reporting to law enforcement, a victim carefully guards her confidentiality, and authorities attempt to protect her name. This is all good and necessary. I get it. But how much of this desire to keep these crimes personal and private comes from living in a society where so many people still have very little understanding of these crimes? How many in our society still want to question the victim's behavior and suggest that she may have caused her own rape? Or believe that her unrelated sexual history somehow played a part in her rape? How many people continue making moral judgments aimed at the victim, thus minimizing and ignoring the action of the rapist? How many people are unable to offer sincere support because their own silence and discomfort are easily sensed by the victim?

It is no wonder we have kept these traumas personal and private. For years, survivors who chose to speak out did so from behind a dark curtain. Their identity was a secret. Why? There is no shame in being the victim of a crime. The shame belongs to the offender, not the victim. In a better world, there would be no need to fear exposure after being the victim of rape. In a better world, there would be the clear recognition and distinction between victim and perpetrator. A victim would not fear lack of support, understanding, and justice. Keeping these crimes personal and private comes very close to encouraging the silence, and encouraging the silence allows the cycle of violence and abuse to continue.

So, going back to my theory, could the misconception that rape has something to do with sex possibly be one reason for the discomfort and unwillingness to engage in conversation regarding this issue? Does it play a role in our silence? Sex gone wrong may be a personal issue. Rape is not.

Our language needs to change. From here on out, I will be using what I believe to be more honest and accurate terms for what we have previously referred to as sexual violence and sexual assault. I will be using the terms "intimate violence" and "intimate assault." It just makes much more sense. Rape is a crime against one's physical, personal, and intimate being. There is nothing sexual about it. The dictionary defines intimate as being *inmost or deep within, pertaining to or characteristic of the inmost or essential nature.* These are crimes of power, control, humiliation, and degradation. The physical assault on a victim's being is horrendous enough, but ask most survivors of intimate assault where their real pain lies; they will tell you it is deep within the most intimate and fragile part of their shattered spirit. These are intimate assaults.

So perhaps, if my theory is correct that the misdirected idea of sex playing a role in these crimes is contributing to our silence, changing our language to more honest terms may slowly allow more comfortable conversation and awareness. We can speak of robbery, murder, kidnapping, car-jacking, physical assault, and every other crime without doing the "squirm." It is time we do the same for intimate violence; it is time the silence stops.

*   *   *

It has been said that when we are able to tell our story, any story, that that story will begin to lose whatever power it has held over us. The story will no longer be bigger and stronger than the individual. The individual will become bigger and stronger than the story. We, as a society, must create an environment where victims will feel emotionally safe to come forward, tell their story, and pursue justice if necessary.

The Story Project, begun in Portland, Oregon by educator, counselor and facilitator Robin Mayther, seems to be a wonderful example of just that. Mayther has created a safe place for our youth to tell their truths, communicate their feelings, and know that they are not alone. As they share their stories and life experiences with their peers and trusted adults, they become stronger and their stories become weaker. Their feelings of pain and isolation transform into feelings of personal strength and confidence. These young survivors are then able to experience the clarity necessary to move forward and make positive choices to live healthier lives.

It's been months, and the darkness continues to follow my every move. I wake up, the darkness wakes up. I turn right, the darkness turns right. I can't be alone with it anymore.

I tell.

I am comforted in the brief conversation. We don't tell others. Too uncomfortable. No more talk about it. Maybe if we don't talk about it, it will go away.

It doesn't.

I don't have the words to help anyone understand how deep into my soul this pain goes. And so there is silence. It's not their fault, they don't know. My silence mirrors their silence. I will fold back up deep within myself. This is the safest place for me. No one can hurt me here. No one can make me feel as though my pain doesn't matter.

There is no healing in the isolation and the silence. One victim's inability to heal will eventually affect society as a whole. When statistics are telling us that one in six women and one in thirty-three men are being intimately assaulted, we need to pay attention. Ignoring the residual emotional effects that these traumas have on their victims only delays healing or inhibits it altogether. We are then left with individuals who might deal with their pain in unhealthy ways. Self-medicating with drugs or alcohol is not uncommon. Turning to unhealthy relationships becomes what they know. Suicidal thoughts come and go, then sometimes are quieted forever. This all tears at and weakens the fabric of our society. The unresolved trauma prevents mothers and fathers from being the best parents they can be. It prevents employees from being the best employees they can be, focused and responsible. We are not the best husband or wife, daughter, son, or friend. We are not our best self when the cloud of pain and isolation constantly hovers over the deep cracks in our spirit.

How is it possible that over thirty years later a memory can still bring me to tears, tears of overwhelming sadness that almost always catch me off guard? It's the grieving process, I know. Because they are the same kind of tears that come when one has lost something so dear and precious—something that will never come back. I lost me.

Bits and pieces of me . . . I wonder who I might have been and what I might have accomplished in my life if not for the darkness that has cluttered my mind. If not for the scars that dimmed the light in my spirit. Would I have been a better me? . . . Perhaps I might have been far beyond this grieving process by now and even further along on my healing journey if it hadn't been for the silence.

Our silence has allowed us to remain naive and perhaps even apathetic to these crimes that know no boundaries. They are happening far too often with disproportionate attention, awareness, and solutions. Society needs to get to a place of outrage and intolerance, a place that has no room for the stillness and discomfort. We are getting there, slowly we are getting there.

*   *   *

"When I arrived home, I told my father and mother what had happened. I will never forget the look of pain in their eyes and the hurt they felt as I begged them not to call the police. I just wanted to forget it happened. I had been drinking underage at a party, and I was accusing the captain of the football team of rape. I didn't want to go through the whole legal process and then lose anyway and be the talk of the town. I didn't want the emotional pain. I truly believed that, in time, the pain would go away, and it would be like it never happened to me. Little did I know that I would not be able to escape the emotional strain it put on my life nor the feeling that part of my life was gone. And I would never get it back. It would be something I would live with forever."

Marissa
Intimate assault survivor

"The look in his eyes will haunt me forever. The more I struggled and fought, the more he seemed to enjoy it. I thought it would never end. I just remember giving up the fight and praying he would finish . . . My body felt dirty and disgusting. Afterward, I promptly took a shower and scrubbed myself as hard as I could. When I got out of the shower, I kept telling myself that it didn't happen. I refused to think about it. As far as I was concerned, it was a nightmare that wasn't real. I didn't tell anyone. Besides, who would have believed me? I wasn't exactly as pure as the driven snow. I couldn't go to the cops. I didn't want the world to know about my personal life. I refused to deal with my rape for three years."

Sarah
Intimate assault survivor

"My father is in prison, serving sixteen years for sexually abusing me and several other children. Like many children who are sexually abused, I didn't say anything. At least not right away. But when my father was accused of touching one of his step-grandchildren I told all. I was angry, and I was hurt. I wish I had been able to put him away earlier."

Tina
Child intimate abuse survivor

"No one witnessed my 'physical' pain except my sister. She and she alone saw the bruises around my neck. I wore turtlenecks until my bruises healed. About the time the bruises healed, I had another physical condition to deal with. I was pregnant. I never said a word, never went to a doctor . . . Time went on and I set aside the past years that were fueled with hate. I vowed I would raise my precious baby girl with love. Life went on without skipping a beat.

End of discussion . . . Now, four decades later, I'm realizing my 'coping' wasn't all that effective."

Dee
Intimate assault survivor

"My boyfriend sexually abused me on a regular basis. He beat me on a regular basis. From the age of fourteen to sixteen I was abused, and everyone knew it. My parents, my sister, my friends, my classmates, and I knew it. No one called the police. No one offered to help. No one . . . I came home with a black eye. I said, 'Mom, look what he did.' She said, 'Here's what we'll say.' What we'll say? Okay, I tripped over the dog, and my face hit the wall. Okay. I thought Max punched me. Didn't I wake up in his front yard? His front yard is where I came to after a blow to the side of my head . . . Before that, [I remember] Max, with a razor blade grazing my vagina, saying he was gonna slice me. Then he let me get dressed. I get punched, knocked out. Back into consciousness, I get up and run to the neighbor's house. She doesn't answer the door. Here comes Max, laughing. Picks me up, throws me over his shoulder. I see her door getting smaller as he carries me back toward the empty house. Almost to Max's yard, and a voice speaks: 'Max!' The neighbor opens her door. Max lets me go. I run to her. I ask to use her phone. She lets me in. I call my mom. 'Mom, I need a ride. Please come and get me.' 'No.' No ride. Won't get in the car to pick me up, too late. Won't drive two miles to pick up the daughter. Okay. She won't pick me up. Max will take me home. 'Thank you for letting me use the phone.' By now Max has decided he is done with me. No more punches, no more torture with razors tonight. What happened? Oh, right. I fell over the dog and hit my face on the wall . . . No one person pointed out anything might be

wrong. *Not my mom, my sister. Not my teacher or my best friend. No one helped me. No rescue. Not for me. For me, we cover it up with a lie. Like it never happened. Their silence spoke vastly of blame . . . Was I not worthy of saving?"*

Aly
Intimate assault survivor

"By the time I was twelve years old, I was being sexually abused by my stepfather . . . I couldn't talk to anyone about my abuse because I was embarrassed and full of shame. I wanted to have a 'normal' dad. My stepfather was very controlling and didn't allow me to participate in the activities that the other kids were involved in. Friendships were not encouraged, and I felt very isolated. I had very little freedom . . . When I was fifteen, I told my mom what my stepfather had been doing. I couldn't really talk to Mom because it was obvious how painful this was to her. My mom was gentle and meek, and in many ways, I was her caretaker and protector."

Anna
Child intimate abuse survivor

"I was around eight years old and was molested by an older man who went to the church my family attended. This continued for at least a year, maybe two. He would come over to visit my parents, and after everyone had gone outside he would come back in to see me. I remember being incredibly uncomfortable and confused, thinking 'This has to be wrong, but this is Brother_____; he goes to church with us' . . . I was always kind of shy to begin with, but some reason, I still cannot figure out what, kept me quiet. My parents were the type that didn't believe much of what I said because I was one of the creative types, always coming up with some story or pretend thing.

Maybe that was why. Maybe it was because the old man scared me . . . It stopped when the old man died. I secretly smiled at his funeral. I remember being relieved, like this enormous weight had been taken off my little shoulders, but I became incredibly quiet, withdrawn, and reserved."

Amy
Child intimate abuse survivor

"He broke into my bottom-floor apartment and waited for me in my bedroom wearing a ski mask, with a ten-inch knife in his hand. In the midst of being raped, humiliated and petrified with fear, I heard a voice that told me, 'GO NOW!' Right at that instant, I fought to get away from him. I don't know how I got the strength or courage to go, but I didn't stop myself and ask questions. I just fought and ran . . . I didn't realize what physical damage had been done to me until I woke up from surgery. All ten inches of that knife entered into my abdomen just below my diaphragm, and my nipple was hanging by a piece of skin. My wrist was cut to the bone, and my other breast had been sliced open six inches. I had run out of the apartment completely naked, bleeding and screaming . . . The neighbors heard and were standing outside, just staring."

Jaime
Intimate assault survivor

"He told me I was special. He told me we had a special relationship and not to tell my siblings. I had to be in about second grade. And every night as he helped me get ready for bed and into my pajamas, my stepfather molested me. He said if I told my mother he'd kill her, and he held up his huge hand in my face to emphasize his size and strength."

A. G.
Intimate assault survivor, child intimate abuse survivor

"They need the support of good men. They need to know that we are on their side and that we are willing to fight, not only privately but publicly, against this violence. Do not be a good man who does nothing, who stays silent and watches as the people we love are harmed. Help create a society where every time this crime is committed, outrage ensues and justice is demanded. Help stop the silence and create a society where women are not blamed for the violent actions of men."

Brandon
Law enforcement advocate for victims of intimate assault

CHAPTER 2

Misconceptions

*I*f you think you do not know a victim of intimate assault you might want to think again. Remember, the estimates are one in six women and one in thirty-three men are intimately assaulted. Accurate statistics are difficult to obtain for many reasons, one being the ongoing silence of generations. Especially statistics regarding child intimate abuse. The silence surrounding these deplorable crimes against our most innocent is particularly profound. But it is this silence that deceives us into thinking we have no connection to the issue. So I say, think again.

Think of your social circle—your family, coworkers, church members, friends, and acquaintances. You know six women. You know twelve, twenty-four, thirty-six women.

At the very least, I can pretty much guarantee you know one or more survivors. And I can pretty much guarantee they are carrying a pain with them that, at times, has left them feeling alone and isolated. Because of our social silence. Because of our lack of awareness and understanding. Because of our misconceptions.

In the previous chapter, I addressed one of the biggest misconceptions regarding intimate assault. The notion that these crimes are about sex. They are not. They are about an extreme disrespect and disregard for another human being. They are about power, control, humiliation, and degradation. I can't say it enough.

I suppose the origin of this particular "it's about sex" misconception is not too difficult to figure out. Many rapes occur during a night of partying. Boy meets girl. It's a seemingly enjoyable time: Conversation, maybe some drinks, some dancing. Flirting? Maybe. She may even offer a hug and a kiss or two. Bits and pieces of the instinctual, human mating game. If the evening is concluding with consensual sex, the "it's about sex" notion applies. If the evening is concluding with a forced intimate assault, the game changes. It no longer has anything to do with sex. It has to do with an individual who cannot take no for an answer. It has to do with someone who has no respect for another's choice over what is done to her body and spirit. The act is born out of power, force, and humiliation. It hardly resembles the enjoyable act of sex.

Perpetrators love using the "mixed messages" excuse. "She was kissing me and dancing real close." Really? That's all it takes for someone to believe he has the right to forcibly take what is not his to take? Since when does kissing or hand holding or a touch mean "I want to have sex with you"? We are not animals, void of reasoning and judgment. We all are capable of using self-control. Some simply choose not to.

* * *

Because there is this misconception about sex playing a part in these crimes, there is also the misconception that it cannot be rape if the victim and offender are in a dating or married relationship. Sex, after all, is an important component to healthy relationships. Consensual sex, that is. But there is no ownership of another's body in any relationship and consent in dating and marriage always matters. If not consensual, the same power, force, and humiliation used to take what is not a partner's to take, leaves the victim feeling as broken as if the offender was unknown.

As an advocate, one of my more heartbreaking intimate assault cases was of a newly married woman, well over fifty years old, who was emotionally and intimately assaulted by her husband. Her painful bruises showed the physical violence he somehow felt entitled to, but it was the look in her eyes and the sound of her voice that told the story of her now-broken spirit. Her husband wasn't having sex with her. Her husband took without consent. Her husband raped her.

* * *

According to a Bureau of Justice Statistics, National Crime Victimization Survey, it is estimated that in 2006, 62 percent of perpetrators were known to their victims in some way. The common misconception that most assaults are committed by the "stranger in the bushes" does not hold true. Nor does the belief that the force of a gun or knife is needed to complete an assault. Verbal intimidation will work just fine, as does the ability of the known offender to gain the victim's trust as he isolates her.

Many victims will feel guilty after the fact, wondering why they were not able to put up more of a fight during their assault, especially those victims who knew their attacker. After all, there was no threat of a frightening gun or knife. Perhaps there is a false sense of security when a victim knows the offender. Normally, we are not thinking that the people we associate with would turn on us so cruelly and betray us. But when one is in the midst of a traumatic event, the mind does not always think logically. Clear-headed thinking can go right out the window. Rape can easily become life threatening, and a surviving victim must believe that whatever action she took or did not take was the right thing to do.

I notice him looking down at me as he starts his slippery descent down the staircase. One minute he's there, the next minute he's not, until his head pops back up at the bottom of the stairs, and he pretty much lands on two feet right in front of my lunch table. Good thing he's not hurt, because I can't help laughing. And neither can he. Funny way to meet a fellow student but definitely a conversation starter . . . Ever since his stumble down the steps, whenever he's passing through the campus cafeteria and sees me, he stops to say hi. Seems like a friendly guy, nice smile . . . He tells me someone is having a party this weekend and says I should think about going. Maybe I will. I'll think about it . . . Why not go? Might be fun and a good chance to meet some other people. Being away from home, I don't really know anyone on campus . . . I drive myself to the party. I walk in and see my new friend standing in the living room. Three other guys

*are with him. I don't know them. No one else is in the house.
It's okay, I'm probably just early, and no one has shown up
yet.*

*   *   *

Few intimate assaults are impulsive acts. The majority
of intimate assaults are premeditated, and studies show that
when multiple assailants are involved in the assault, there is
a greater likelihood that the assault was planned.

The perpetrator is just looking for the right opportunity.
And he gets very clever at recognizing it. He will know a
vulnerable victim when he sees one. He will look for and
recognize the traits that will consciously allow him to take
advantage of his victim.

The harmless innocent and those so willing to trust,
unintentionally allowing victim isolation, can make easy
targets. As do the individuals who have already been
broken and groomed over time into people who feel little
self-worth—perhaps as a result of having been raised
in a home where the constant reinforcement of negative
self-beliefs was commonplace. The young (or old) female
(or male) intoxicated from "one too many" becomes a fairly
effortless opportunity for someone to take what is not his
(or hers) to take.

I see these scenarios time and time again as I work with
victims of intimate assault; not one of these scenarios in any
way justifies the horrific action of the rapist. It is clear to
me that the perpetrators know who they are looking for, and
they know well before they act.

*I don't know what evil looks like. I've never been
exposed to evil. At eighteen, my world is still small and*

narrow, comfortable and safe. I am well-loved by my parents, receiving all the attention and care I need—even in a busy home filled with my five brothers and three sisters. I'm a compliant, easy teen, still holding onto the sweet, naive innocence of a child. My world has been a good world, a simple world.

*   *   *

"She was asking for it" is one of the most common misconceptions, and we hear it often. It goes hand in hand with victim-blaming. Why we would want to dismiss the actions of the rapist and focus on the dress and behavior of the victim is beyond me. The offender cares little about the clothing or lack of. Many convicted offenders cannot even remember what their victim looked like or what she was wearing.

There are those who believe a female who was drinking and partying "had it coming." No, she did not. Drinking does not imply consent and is not a pass for someone to simply take. Some states have very clear laws that state if a perpetrator knows or should know the victim is mentally or physically unable to resist or give consent (too drunk, too drugged, or mentally handicapped), he is guilty of intimate assault. A rapist is not looking for a pleasant, sexual encounter. He is focused on the opportunity and the vulnerability of a victim. He is motivated by anger, power, and control. The offender is solely responsible for his own actions. She did not ask for it.

I'm wearing a long-sleeved, brown turtleneck sweater, camel-colored pants I proudly made myself, and brown knee-high boots. Never really think of myself as sexy.

Certainly not tonight. The only flesh showing on my body is my face and hands. I'm safe.

*   *   *

If you were to believe television and movie dramas that portray intimate assault victims as having hysterical and highly emotional reactions to their crime, it is not surprising that misconceptions regarding the victim's believability abound. The truth is, most victims of intimate assault often immediately present themselves in a much calmer manner than is depicted in television dramas. The shock, emotional numbness, and humiliation can be disguised as a calmness. They may use denial as a shield against the trauma. "If I smile and pretend I'm okay, maybe it will all go away." It is not at all unusual for a victim who is in the midst of her forensic rape exam to share a smile and even a soft laugh with her nurse and advocate. Few are hysterical, few are emotionally uncontrollable. On the contrary, they exhibit an unexpected control in hopes that it will keep in check a pain that cuts deep. Their affect is actually the exact opposite of what we would assume a victim's affect would be.

You may have read about high-profile cases that make the news, accusing well-known people of intimate assault. The victims may not have reported the crime for quite some time, but when they do, their behavior around the time of the alleged assault is closely scrutinized. People are looking for proof of the emotionally distraught victim: the hysterical behavior, the tears. When those behaviors are not noted, it is assumed the assault must not have happened.

Precious children who are being intimately abused go to school day after day while in the midst of their abuse. They get good at hiding their pain. They smile and laugh, and no one knows. Battered women put on their "happy faces" along with make-up to cover the bruises and go off to work. Not the behavior we would assume from a victim of a serious crime. But not all is as it seems.

If you are looking for obvious and visible physical wounds to prove an intimate assault, forget it. Most injuries are easily hidden. Sometimes the physical injury can be minimal and heal quickly. The emotional wounds are a different story. The fact that there was not any dramatic, physical injury does not mean there was not an assault. If you believe otherwise, you are watching too much television.

We need to understand that the initial reaction (or lack of reaction) from a victim cannot be the gauge for determining whether or not an assault has occurred. Their emotions are far too complex and are unique to each individual. There is no "right way" to respond to rape.

No red flags are waving back and forth in my head, but what do I know? I was never a party girl in high school, so this is new to me. Still, I think at least a few others would be here by now . . . But there's no loud party music playing on the stereo, no chips and dip or pretzels for guests to munch on. I'm not noticing any drinks around nor am I even offered one. Yet no dread crosses my mind. My innocence tells me I'm just an early bird, others will be coming soon . . . It happens quickly. I'm not in that house ten minutes before my world stops making sense. They are telling me to get into the bedroom. They tell me to undress. I am instantly alone in my fear. I am as small and insignificant as a person can possibly be. I don't understand. What is happening? There are four of them and one of me. I do as they say. I have lost myself in fear and confusion. I am not trying to run. I am not screaming for help. I am not kicking, scratching, or hitting. I am not there. Except for the tears streaming down my face, I am not there. One by one they take their turn, each patiently waiting at the foot of the bed to take my spirit and crush it into tiny, unrecognizable pieces.

*   *   *

The misconceptions that swirl around the issue of false accusations seem to be an ongoing dilemma. The statistics, often inconsistent, seem to be of little help. Studies will show that anywhere from 2 percent to 50 percent of rape allegations are false. That's quite a large gap. The most reliable study results seem to indicate a range of 4 percent to 8 percent.

The problem with so many different studies may be that there is an inconsistency in the definition of rape in some legislative areas. Language plays a big part in the inaccuracies. "False accusations" could mean an accuser did, in fact, lie about the assault, or it could mean the accuser made an honest mistake in identifying her rapist. Falsely identifying the offender does not mean the crime did not happen. Studies do not always distinguish between the two, nor do they take into account victims who choose to drop charges or not cooperate with the case. Cases filed away as "unfounded" or "baseless" do not mean the crime did not happen.

Time and time again, I speak with victims who are frustrated with the legal process. They tell me police and detectives are not acting as though they believe their story (certainly not the case with all law enforcement), which, of course, is not helpful in the healing process. Victims may fear exposure and retaliation from the offender and his supporters. Or they may battle the problematic "he said, she said." And unless the evidence is undeniable, with credible witnesses willing to come forward (how often are there witnesses to rape?), the case becomes weak. Victims simply want to be done with their emotional rollercoaster. The case is dropped, neatly put away. It is unfortunate that the victim cannot put her rape away as neatly.

There are far too many variables in these unscientific studies, and the discrepancies make my head spin. I can only speak of what I know to be true. To be falsely accused of intimate assault—or any other crime—is detestable and can unfairly turn someone's world upside down. But it is interesting to me that the headline of a false accusation quite often gets far more attention and social outrage than the issue of intimate violence itself. What I know to be true is that there are far more victims of these horrific crimes than there are false accusations. Far more. Not many females choose to entertain the idea of repeated questioning by law enforcement, signing legal affidavits ensuring all that they are speaking the truth, and the uncomfortable, invasive, physical forensic exam.

One falsely accused person is one too many. But believing that most intimate assaults are false accusations is wrong, and will not make the issue go away. It is akin to burying your head in the sand, giving us the false sense of security that these crimes really are not happening all that often. They are. And our denial is what the offenders are depending on as they move toward their next victim.

* * *

The misconception that men don't get raped is, unfortunately, false. Men do get raped. One in thirty-three if you go by the 2006 National Violence Against Women

Survey. Heterosexual men and gay men are raped. It is believed that the reporting rate for male rapes is even lower than that for female rapes. The reasons seem obvious, as the embarrassment and humiliation are so profound. Yet how are these feelings able to be processed when we raise the males in our society to be so emotionally stoic? We discourage our little boys from crying when they feel like crying. We try to raise tough little men that grow up into tough, strong men. Strong men should be able to fight off their rapist. But we know that is not always possible. And because intimate assaults are more a crime against our spirit than they are against our physical being, males have a very difficult time processing their emotions. The resulting emotional trauma is significant.

As with female victims, we must create accessible resources where males will feel emotionally safe enough to speak out and begin the long healing process. Male support groups can do that. They must know they are not alone in their experience. Isolating or attempting to ignore this particular trauma can hamper the healing process, turning unresolved anger and pain into unhealthy life choices, including excessive alcohol use, drug use, thoughts of suicide, and anger issues.

*   *   *

"In the fall of 1980, a part of me died . . . I was at a party with my boyfriend. He had been drinking, and we got into an argument. All I wanted to do was leave. One of his friends offered to give me a ride home. I grabbed my things and left with him. Instead of taking the turn to my house, he turned down a road that took us back to where we would sometimes go four-wheeling. I told him I wasn't in the mood

---

to go four-wheeling and I just wanted to go home, but he insisted. He said he wanted to give me time to calm down and sober up before I went home. I knew I had only had a couple beers and was fine to go home. But he didn't take me home, and the next thing I knew we hit a tree . . . Instead of asking me if I was all right, he said he was going to rape me. I instantly reached for the door handle, got out, and began to run. The next thing I knew, I was being tackled to the ground and being hit, and my clothes were being torn . . . I lay there and felt a part of me die."

Marissa
Intimate assault survivor

"I'm not sure how the conversation started, it was so long ago. My sister, two aunts, mother, dad, and I were in the living room at my parent's home. Somehow we got on the subject of rape. My father told us a story about how he got "frisky" one night with a girl, and she let him know in no uncertain terms that she wasn't having it. That had convinced my father that unless there was a weapon, a girl couldn't be raped. A girl could and can fight off her would-be rapist . . . I snapped! Right there in my parent's living room I lost it. I remember shouting, 'So you think I lied? All these years, you think I lied?' I remember seeing the horrified look on everyone's faces . . . You see, I wasn't held at knife or gunpoint, nothing so dramatic. My head was bashed against a wooden couch armrest while my rapist strangled me . . . The fear of dying is as powerful as the gun or knife. I was afraid to die. But I have died in so many ways since."

Dee
Intimate assault survivor

"The abuse did not happen overnight. I was prepped for it. Groomed. Set up by a culture that begins the process of breaking the spirit of women early. So, by the age of ten, I was a broken spirit. I had no rights to my body, my mind, or my soul. My stepfather saw to that. He moved in and began to methodically destroy my will, break my spirit, and reduce my self-esteem to the point of complete surrender. It began with words like 'stupid' and 'conceited.' The first time I was hit by him I didn't cry. I began to count. Each time I got hit, I added one more number. Eventually I lost count. My sister and my mother would plead with me. 'Don't do anything wrong. Please.' But I would mess up, as kids do. I was the cause of so much pain and suffering. Me, a little girl. I was garbage, less than nothing, ugly . . . It was not until many years later that I understood how a victim instinctively knows the predator. If I believe I am a piece of shit, it is normal to seek out people who treat me like shit. I never thought I was of value. By fourteen, my spirit was broken so badly I accepted whatever was dished out to me. I was in agreement that I was stupid, ugly, and just so unworthy of love that pain was all I would ever get . . . His name was Max. He was verbally abusive, but I accepted that as normal. It was what I knew, never questioning that there was no truth in what he or my stepdad said . . . At fourteen, fifteen, and sixteen years old I was beaten, raped, and tortured, and I did not resist. I endured this and didn't fight. I agreed to be abused. How does a person accept that kind of treatment without defending herself?"

Aly
Intimate assault survivor

"I'm horribly self-conscious and wear a happy mask when I'm at work so that people won't ask me about my personal life."

Amy
Child intimate abuse survivor

"I had known the man who attacked me, and so did my neighbors. He lived right there in the same apartment complex. I had spoken with him in passing. I even knew his first name . . . My hope is that someday, when a person commits such a crime and is convicted, he will not be allowed to live so freely. I get angry when I hear of someone being attacked by a criminal who is a previous offender, which is what happened to me. The statistics for rehabilitation of sex offenders are not hopeful, and I do not feel they justify what seems to be the typical lenient punishment . . . I can only be thankful for how things worked out when it came to the court process and sentencing for this criminal. I know I am one of the lucky victims that received as much earthly justice as possible. It's unnerving to know that our society expects convicted sex offenders to register themselves when they are out of prison. That somehow they can be trusted to check in when they have moved from place to place. Since when is a criminal an honorable person?"

Jaime
Intimate assault survivor

"I think it's interesting that most folks don't really realize that people who do these kinds of things to children look 'normal.' Child rapists and molesters look like anyone and can prey upon any child in a vulnerable position."

Allecia
Child intimate abuse survivor

"I was helping a friend of the family work on his car. My mother was out of town, and my older brother was watching me. But my brother had gone to play basketball, and I was left in the hands of our friend. He was nineteen and like an older brother to me. I was twelve . . . He tried to hold me down as we fought, but I managed to fight myself onto the concrete and ran like heck. He chased me until I was able to safely run into our apartment. By then my brother had returned home. Our dear family friend then whispered to me through the door that he only did it to show me what he didn't want any other guy to do to me. He was just 'showing me a lesson.' He said he was sorry. He said he didn't mean to hurt me."

A. G.

Intimate assault survivor, child intimate abuse survivor

"The abuse and molestation were the most damaging. They happened at a very young age, when I was trusting of the father figure. He was someone I trusted and looked up to. Because he folded his relationship with me into his affection and adoration for me, I was under a misconception of trust and what a relationship really meant. He planted a sense of badness and guilt within my spirit that I was innately bad. But I wasn't. I was a very good little girl. I was most lovable and trusting. He used that to his advantage."

A. G.

Intimate assault survivor, child intimate abuse survivor

"I knew the three guys. The one who actually raped me was a family friend. I'd known him since fifth grade. One of the other guys I didn't really know as well . . . My heart sank as I saw the third guy sitting shotgun in the car. He was my best friend since ninth grade. He was like a brother to me. I

was numb, feeling overwhelmed with his betrayal. My best friend did nothing to protect me, he was part of it . . . It took me years to realize this was rape. A premeditated rape. I couldn't acknowledge it as rape, because these were guys I knew; they were not strange men with masks on in the dark. I knew them . . . But friends don't do this to us."

Nanette
Intimate assault survivor

"Several years ago, I accompanied a young man to the hospital ER. He had been sexually assaulted, and he needed to be cared for. I remember he was crying, and the hospital staff looked at him with doubt as if to say, 'We don't believe you were raped. You couldn't really have been victimized, because you're a guy.' They basically told him to go home, take an aspirin, and sleep it off. They were not at all interested in the emotional trauma this young man had just experienced. Not to mention the possibility of physical injury or STDs (sexually transmitted diseases). *This was a victim, who was victimized again by their indifference. I had wanted to be by his side so he knew someone stood with him; it was at my encouragement that he wanted to report it at all. Searching out the help he needed was meant to value him, but it ended up devaluing him . . . This young man was not alone in his experience. I have supported other males, gay and straight, who knew they were not believed, and it was a blow to their self-esteem. What strikes me now and saddens me as I think about this is the betrayal and pain in their eyes. It is just one more chink in whatever amount of self-esteem they might have had. It is a mixture of betrayal and resignation, as if they are saying to themselves, 'What do I expect? I am already looked down on; who really cares?'*

"I feel there is still a mental mind-set in our society to diminish the real impact of sexual assault in our communities considering the way we currently collect statistical data, omitting swaths of victims. It is used to shroud and minimize the reality."

Ben
Advocate for victims of intimate assault

"The way I see it, there is no crime more hateful than sexual assault. A murderer goes forth and seeks to damage a person's life. A rapist goes forth and seeks to damage a person's soul. It is the most unthinkable type of violence."

Brandon
Law enforcement advocate for victims of intimate assault

CHAPTER 3

Conversation

*T*wo conversations in one week regarding the issue of intimate violence is a pretty good run. Normally the silence is deafening, or if the subject is even broached, it will be changed in the blink of an eye to the all-important weather forecast. But I actually had conversations with two different people on two different days in one week.

The first conversation was with a friendly gentleman who seemed very interested in the informational materials I happened to be handing out at an outreach event. This event was focusing on the problem of homelessness in our community, and the materials I was handing out were resources provided by our local crisis center. He seemed genuinely interested in all the services we provided, including the work we do with victims of intimate assault. We began a conversation.

This nice man had quite a few questions for my partner Shelly and I. Shelly was our crisis center outreach coordinator at the time. She is a gentle spirit, soft-spoken but with a special way of presenting the other side of an issue with clarity and compassion. She calmly educates. I, on the other hand, have a tendency to pounce. Not the best tactic to use while trying to influence a positive change in social attitudes. So I was grateful for Shelly's presence, and I followed her lead of calmness as we conversed with this man.

Most of the conversation centered around one particular question that jumped out at us. He wanted to know what information we presented to the young ladies at our outreaches at the different schools in our area. Did we teach them how to keep themselves safe? Did we talk to them about their behavior, choice of clothing, etcetera? Shelly and I immediately locked eyes for just a split second, hoping we were being discreet so as not to offend this nice man whose questions were sincere and well-meaning. We knew it was our chance to help this gentleman understand a few things. But it was all I could do not to pounce.

My second conversation that week was with a female coworker who was new to my department. This woman seemed to be an intelligent, well-educated woman—pleasant and married with both a son and daughter in college.

On this particular day, work was extremely slow, so we had some time to chat and get to know each other. Our conversation began when she asked me about my volunteer work as an advocate for victims of intimate assault. She seemed mildly curious and asked a few questions, appearing to be shocked when finding out that rape was occurring so often in our society. She admitted she did not like hearing about those things and just did not want to know about it because it was so upsetting.

But the conversation did go on long enough for her to tell me she believed it was the responsibility of the young women who are raped to keep themselves safe and check their behavior. She told me those young women dress in a way that says they are "asking for it," and they should think about the consequences of their actions. Meaning rape. No matter how I tried to point out that only the perpetrator is responsible for his criminal behavior, she would not have it. She insisted both the victim and the perpetrator held responsibility for the rape. As my insides did a slow burn, and although desperately wanting to pounce, I remained cool and calm on the outside, knowing the work place was not the arena to continue this particular conversation.

My coworker was right about one thing. Rape is upsetting and never a pleasant topic of conversation. But pulling down the shade of oblivion is not going to make these crimes go away, nor is it the way to ensure our world becomes a safer place for the youth of our future generations. I imagine perpetrators are quite pleased with this lack of social conversation and interest. No annoying spotlight casting unwanted attention on them. But intimate violence knows no boundaries, and wearing blinders is hardly an effective way to bring about much-needed change and awareness for society as a whole.

Although these two conversations left me feeling somewhat frustrated (we'll get to their common theme of victim-blaming later), I am still so grateful for them. Whether or not I agree with the opinions of others, or whether or not they agree with me, at least we are having conversations. And that means we are stopping the silence. Anything to stop the paralyzing silence is a step forward. Conversation can do that. Conversation can slowly melt away the obvious discomfort society has regarding the subject of intimate violence. The more we talk, the less uncomfortable it will be to begin the process of creating positive change.

Conversations are eye-openers for all engaged. Information is received. Information is given. What was once misunderstood can become understood. We experience it every day with our many different relationships. A good conversation leaves us knowing more, understanding more.

Bringing change of any sort must first start with a mindful consciousness that something is not right, that something is terribly unfair and unjust. These thoughts must then turn into conversation, words that will awaken an awareness in others, compelling decent people to take action. Conversation and knowledge can do that.

*   *   *

"Society seems so blind to rape. And I was no different. It never crossed my mind. I never believed it could happen to me."

Marissa
Intimate assault survivor

"When I started school, my teachers would call my parents and write on my report card that I had a short attention span and that I wouldn't pay attention in class. I would fall asleep in class and was easily distracted and bored. My social skills were delayed, and I was a poor student. I remember feeling different from the other students and embarrassed because I didn't do well in school. A few teachers made home visits in an effort to see if anything was unusual at home. But

everything always seemed quite normal there. I had two well-behaved brothers and a sweet, loving, stay-at-home mother who kept a clean and cozy home. One teacher even came over for dinner to assess the home environment, but nothing ever came of that . . . Nothing was said about what he was doing to me . . .

As a teenager, my anger turned to hate, and I started having horrible nightmares. My nightmares were about killing my stepfather and putting an end to his sexual and emotional abuse. Every night, as soon as I closed my eyes, I would start dreaming about how I could kill him. I was consumed with hate and anger. We didn't have a gun in the house, so most of the time in my dreams I was stabbing him with a knife or giving him poison. When I would wake up from these dreams, my childlike, immature thoughts never told me that it would be wrong to kill him or that I would go to prison. I always thought that the police would understand my suffering and that I would finally be protected by them and that I would be able to stay with my mom. I thought the police would see how horrible he was and that everything would be okay if he died. The 'killing nightmares' stopped after I moved out after graduation . . . I was a gentle kid, a sensitive kid who always protected the underdog. I was polite and never mean to anyone. If I would have killed my stepfather, I most likely would have spent the rest of my life in prison. No one would have known what he was doing to me and probably wouldn't have believed me. This is what bothers me when I hear of children who kill their abusive parents. These children are fragile, and in these situations, they can be pushed to the breaking point. Any child can kill when pushed to this painful breaking point. These children need a voice and need to be protected. People need to know what is really happening to children. It breaks my heart when I hear about the way these kids are treated and that they think of themselves as damaged goods. I wish the public could know and understand that these kids are not 'bad seeds.' They are innocent children who were abused, day in and day out, and were pushed to explosive violence. I had those dreams, and yet I am the most peaceful person I know; the most important thing in my life is peace. There is nothing violent about me."

Anna
Child intimate abuse survivor

"It was probably close to two years since I had really thought about how I was being affected by the whole ordeal. I had moved back home with my family, and about that same time, I found myself in the throes of what I would call a breakdown. Even though I knew I was surrounded by people who loved me, I felt more alone than I ever had before. I couldn't help but remember that they really had no idea how it felt for me. They knew they could only imagine. They were scared for me, and they were horrified, but only I really knew what it was like to have been through that horrific night. That made me feel so very alone. I could see it on the people's faces who knew what had happened to me: they couldn't tell if they should ask how I was doing, or if it was safer to just not say anything . . . At one point, the counselor I had been meeting with before I moved had called me to see how I was doing, and I happened to be in the midst of an anxiety attack. I shared with her what was going on in my head regarding this battle, how I felt abandoned by God. All she had to say was, 'Go to the ER so you can get some medication to help you calm down.' I never spoke to her again."

Jaime
Intimate assault survivor

"I was raped by my father, my mother, and several of their friends. My brother was also abused in this way, but I have never been able to speak to him about what he remembers or experienced . . . I have things that have happened to me by my mother that I cannot tell anyone. There are no words for the things she made me do when I was a child."

Allecia
Child intimate abuse survivor

"Until we acknowledge that this happens, how can we begin the conversation and discuss this act of violence? We need people to wake up and realize that this happens and it's happening to your daughters, your wives, your mothers, your sisters, and your cousins. Think about how many people have done the assaulting—they want us to stay silent. The more we stay silent, the more power we are giving them to continue this behavior. How many more women need to be assaulted before we say enough is enough?"

Nanette
Intimate assault survivor

CHAPTER 4

Victim-Blaming

*I*t troubles me greatly to know that victims of intimate assault still remain hesitant to report these deplorable crimes. According to the US Department of Justice, 2005 National Crime Victimization Study, roughly 60 percent of victims will not go to law enforcement. Many will not tell family and friends. These are crimes that cause immeasurable humiliation, degradation, and embarrassment. The resulting emotional pain cuts deep. It is unacceptable that we live in a society unwilling to see rape for exactly what it is.

I don't know what they think. I don't know if a part of them blames a part of me. I don't know because of the silence, because of the absent conversation. But I do know

I cannot and do not blame myself for what was done to me. That is forever clear in my head. I will not even criticize my unsophisticated and youthful trust in others that took me to that darkest night, and it saddens me that my once unspoiled notion of trust now bears its black mark. Those four guys chose their actions very carefully without any help from me. No piece of that evil night belongs to me . . . except for my silence.

The two conversations I spoke of in the last chapter are indicative of a social attitude that many people continue to accept. The tiresome comments about what a particular person was wearing, or what he or she was drinking, who they were with, or where they were, hold no merit when determining who is responsible for committing the crime of rape. If, as my coworker suggests, the victim is partly responsible for the crime because she had too much cleavage showing and was "asking for it," are we then excusing the perpetrator for his actions? Are we giving him a pass? Are we saying he really couldn't help himself—that it had to be her fault? Do we honestly believe that we as human beings have so little self-control that the sight of another's flesh causes us to rape?

It is interesting that my husband and the husbands of my girlfriends have not yet turned into rapists. God knows they have seen their share of cleavage. They have even seen women partying into the wee hours of the morning, high on the drink. But they did not rape. They did not rape because intimate assault has nothing to do with the behavior of the intended victim. Rapists rape because they alone make that choice. There is no sharing the responsibility with the victim.

It has been noted in the past that when high-profile rape cases are reported in the news and the "alleged" victim's personal history is exposed, reports of other intimate assaults decrease in number. And why not? Who would want to report a rape believing so much of their personal life will become everyone else's business? Not only does the rape traumatize them to their core, but now they take on the struggle of moral judgment by others.

Perhaps society is erroneously using moral judgment when it comes to determining if one is a victim of rape or not. But moral judgment has no place here. It is because of this unfair social bias that the rape shield laws were introduced in the late 1970s and early 1980s. The rape shield laws attempt to protect the victim from irrelevant information being presented as evidence at trial, information such as sexual history, reputation, or past conduct, which have no bearing on the specific incident being judged. They attempt to ensure the victim is treated with respect and dignity. I say "attempt" because they have not always proven to be foolproof. What they cannot ensure is public opinion and judgment outside the courtroom. They cannot protect the victim from the media and all the personal information it chooses to report.

Some time ago, I was following up with an intimate assault victim I had helped as she was going through her forensic rape exam. I called her a couple of days after the exam, wanting to know how she was doing. Not surprisingly, she was still very upset, angry, and trying to process what had happened—all reasonable and healthy emotions. She told me she had confided in her boss (female) at work and explained to her a bit about what she had been through. Her boss reacted with, "What were you doing out on a Thursday night?"

I am willing to give her boss the benefit of the doubt and assume she did not ask that question with any evil intent, but I can assure you painful damage was done. Beside the fact that the question was insensitive and had absolutely no bearing on the assault, her boss implied that the victim was somewhat responsible for her own assault simply because she was out on a Thursday night. A more appropriate and thoughtful question the boss could have asked was, "How could and why would someone harm another person in such a hurtful and disrespectful way?"

The boss's comment is a perfect example of a pervasive lack of understanding and knowledge regarding intimate assault. These kinds of comments can keep victims silent, unwilling to risk the unfair judgment and accusatory, off-the-cuff remarks. It is pain on top of pain and serves no purpose.

Insinuating that a rape victim is to blame for her own rape based on her morals or standard of living is unfair and unjust. It is illogical. The young woman out partying it up until three in the morning does not deserve to be raped. A hangover? Perhaps. Raped? No. That cute, young lady out and about in her tiny little mini-skirt and low-cut T-shirt does not deserve to be raped. On a cold day, the most she deserves is to catch a chill. Raped? No. The prostitute and those considered too promiscuous by someone else's standards do not deserve to be raped. The victim-blaming scenarios can go on and on. We can pitch the blame every which way to try to distort the reality. But it is the rapist alone who carries the blame.

More than once, I have been at the side of a young teenage girl who decided she would sneak out of the house to meet up with friends, knowing her parents would probably not approve. By the end of the evening she has become a victim of intimate assault. For many, including the parents, their first thought might be *she wouldn't have been raped if she hadn't been where she wasn't supposed to be.* But that is not true. The truth is, she was raped only because of someone else's decision to rape. The fact that she made a foolish decision to sneak out of the house does not transfer responsibility of the crime from perpetrator to victim. Rape is never ever the appropriate consequence for anyone's foolish behavior.

I am careful as I speak with overwhelmed, upset parents, encouraging them to clearly understand the separate issues and deal with them accordingly. Their teen snuck out of the house. Their teen was raped. Two separate issues. Their child has been violated and is already full of self-blame. Their most important job right now is to be a loving, safe place for their child. A place of support. The teen's foolish behavior of sneaking out of the house, of course, should be addressed at some point and dealt with appropriately. But the teen's foolish behavior and subsequent assault are two separate issues, not to be confused.

I do not deny there are many foolish behaviors that put us at risk for possible harm. But foolish behavior does not determine whether or not we deserve to be the victim of a crime or that we are responsible for that crime. I can think of no other crime where the victim is put under such personal scrutiny as in a rape case. I can think of no other crime where the victim is hesitant to report for fear of unnecessary humiliation or embarrassment, or even the possibility of not being believed. Those people who leave their windows open on a warm summer night do not expect or deserve to be robbed blind, but they are. We are warned time and time again about the consequences of open windows and unlocked doors. Foolish behavior? Perhaps. But we do not seem to blame the robbery victims. They are not shamed into silence. These victims will report to law enforcement without hesitation.

Take that same young woman out partying at night with her short skirt and skimpy top and change the crime against her from rape to pretty much any other crime: robbery, car-jacking, or, God forbid, murder. We now no longer seem as concerned with her behavior, past or present, when she is a victim of other crimes. We no longer scrutinize her morals or look for reasons to blame her for being a victim. We rarely ask what she must have done wrong to cause her own victimization. The crime will be reported without reluctance, since there is little fear of personal judgment. Rape deserves nothing less than the same consideration as any other crime.

When we blame the victim, we seem to be automatically dismissing and minimizing the criminal behavior of the perpetrator. At the same time, the emotional trauma inflicted on the victim has been dismissed and minimized. It is no wonder that the cycle of silence continues—as does the cycle of violence.

I will never understand why we, as a society, would even consider shifting the blame. Why do we put so much energy into trying to figure out what the victim did to deserve the rape? Perhaps victim-blaming is a great avoidance tactic used by society to keep from having to examine the reality and the frequency of intimate violence. This avoidance can naively and blindly keep us in our safe, protected comfort zone. If we do not acknowledge it, we can believe it is not happening. And if we believe it is not happening, we do not have to do anything about it. Perhaps a personal and honest examination of one's inclination to blame the victim would reveal the reasoning behind this very misguided notion.

I can only surmise what I have believed for many, many years: the generations of profound silence surrounding the issue of intimate violence have prevented an accurate understanding of these crimes. It has limited what we know to be true of these crimes. Without the knowledge, understanding, and a conscientious awareness, we will be unable to create the social change necessary to stop the violence.

* * *

"I ran and made my way over to a girlfriend's house where the other girls had met up after the party. I told them what had happened to me. I was standing there, beat up, with my clothes torn. I could tell they didn't believe me. He was on the football team. I was a liar. I felt like trash . . . We all had been in classes that taught us about the dangers of rape. They knew this happened. They did not want to associate my rape with what they had learned. That meant it could also happen to them. Instead it was easier for them to believe I couldn't have been raped. Whatever happened had to be my fault."

Marissa
Intimate assault survivor

"I'm hoping this will finally bring me closure. I'm hoping that someday I can trust men again. But most importantly, I hope that this will open people's eyes. Victims of sexual assault and abuse should not be made to feel guilty. It is not our fault. We did not ask for any of it . . . If you are a victim, please realize it was not your fault. You did not deserve it. If you've never been violated, please understand that this is a traumatic experience that takes forever to heal."

Sarah
Intimate assault survivor

"I always knew I was not to blame for my abuse. And no one ever blamed me. I knew when I was being sexually abused that it was wrong on the part of the abuser. I never blamed myself or felt any kind of personal guilt. The feelings that were most dominant were rage, anger, and a profound sadness. I was an extremely depressed child. My behaviors as a child reflected that, and when I look at pictures of myself as a child I see I appeared depressed . . . I have two brothers I was close to, and I really admired them. They didn't blame me for anything; they simply didn't seem to believe me."

Anna
Child intimate abuse survivor

"No one ever deserves to be victimized nor 'asks for it'—regardless of circumstances. I know I've thought of hundreds of ways how I might have possibly changed something so that I would never have been attacked. But it doesn't matter, because I can't nor can anyone else change what happened to me. A predator is a predator regardless of who, where, when, or why they happen to choose their victim . . . People who don't understand say very stupid things."

Jaime
Intimate assault survivor

"I'm thirty-nine, and for the last twelve years I have had no contact with anyone in my family. The last time I spoke to my father, he disowned me. I guess the confrontation of holding him accountable for his actions was too much. He would rather shut me out of his life forever than help me heal from what he'd done to me."

Allecia
Child intimate abuse survivor

"I've had to work on feeling pretty, sexy, and female. I felt like a boy, feeling masculine for years, because I couldn't take on that gentler, softer side of the female. I felt I always had to be on the defense, to be strong and independent. That was what I had to do for my survival. A career in modeling, acting, and singing and having two daughters forced me to work on finding that feminine side of myself without feeling I'd be taken advantage of or that I was wrong or bad for wanting to look nice. The whole thing with fashion and taking care of myself was a bit self-consuming, and I had a hard time placing attention on myself, on my body. It made me feel guilty and dirty. I didn't know how to blend self-love and care with the sense of sensuality that comes with being a confident female. I had to not feel guilty for attracting the opposite sex."

A. G.

Intimate assault survivor, child intimate abuse survivor

"I made myself my own victim. No one else had to blame me. I did that on my own."

Nanette

Intimate assault survivor

"Murderers and rapists. As a society we seem to lump these people into the same category, that being the worst of humanity. They are put into special populations in prison, and people regard them as evil. The media and people in general acknowledge that these perpetrators have done terrible things to their fellow humans and speak of the perpetrators as fiends and monsters. So, if these perpetrators are generally regarded as villains, why then does much of society continue to look for blame in the victim of sexual crimes? Questioning her clothing.

Questioning her behavior. Questioning her alcohol or drug intake. Bringing up her sexual past during an investigation and trial. A murder victim's behavior is not questioned, so why is the behavior of a rape victim questioned? Yes, the sex organs are involved during the criminal act, and sex, for some, is still taboo to talk about. But society must not allow rapists to go free while their murderous counterparts are eagerly convicted by that same society. Those of us who have survived a sexual assault know too well that a piece of our self was killed when we were violated. Now we must educate humanity so others realize it, too."

Ida
Intimate assault survivor

"This senseless violence has nothing to do with what your survivor was wearing or whether she had a flirty disposition. It has nothing to do with whether or not they had been drinking or if they have had sexual relationships in the past. That is all irrelevant. This has only to do with the sick and twisted monster who believed he had the right to take something that did not belong to him. He is the only one to blame, the only one whose integrity should be questioned."

Brandon
Law enforcement advocate for victims of intimate assault

CHAPTER 5

Long-Term Emotional Aftermath

*S*everal years ago, I came to realize there was a quiet, common thread that connected many survivors of intimate assault and abuse. Recently this realization became even clearer as I searched out conversations with survivors while preparing to write this book. What was expressed to me time and time again was this: When it's "over," it's not over. When one has survived the actual physical and intimate assault, or when the abuse one has endured as a child has stopped, the toughest part is just beginning. It is in this long-term emotional aftermath that the true struggle to survive begins. And it can often be a very lonely, isolated journey. This piece of the intimate violence puzzle is probably the most troubling to me and perhaps the driving force behind my need to write and rant. These are crimes that leave their victims with a scarred soul, but it is a scar no one can see. No one can see when that wound tears open again. No one can see the triggers that send a survivor reeling back to that dark place. Since victims are very good in their attempt to blend back into their normal life, the emotional aftermath isn't obvious to society in general. Within a very short period of time, a victim can appear to be functioning quite well. No one would know the difference. Except the victim.

They are letting me go, and they don't even seem concerned about the consequences. They must know. They must know my humiliation and embarrassment will keep me silent. They must know the degradation has taken hold, and I will tell no one . . . I am numb as I drive myself home in a fog of denial, but the denial is working for me. I go through the motions of steering, shifting, braking. Slow down, remember, you're okay, you're okay . . . I'm home now, and I don't have to think about it anymore. It's over and I'm okay . . . But I'm not okay. I am hurting. What did they do to me? I check my pain with the mirror. I see the tear and the bit of bright, red blood. But my denial is staying faithful to me and I tell myself, "You'll be fine, you're okay, it's going to heal and you'll be just fine." . . . I'll go to work tomorrow as usual, and the day after that is Monday, so I'll be back in class. Nothing has to change, because I'm just fine.

It troubles me to observe that this long-term, emotional struggle has been overlooked or misunderstood at best. If society had a better understanding of the true long-term, emotional harm set upon the victims of these crimes, would social attitudes adjust accordingly? Would our legal and justice systems make serious efforts to put more offenders behind bars? Would punishments equitably begin to fit the crime? How must it feel for the survivor to know that her offender has served his questionably just sentence and is back on the street (often to repeat his criminal behavior) free to live his life? Meanwhile, that same survivor continues the struggle to free her mind of nightmares and to put the pieces of her spirit back together. It makes no sense that the victim is sentenced to far longer time than the offender.

The physical act of intimate assault is terrifying enough even when the victim is spared the bruising or the blood. One can probably imagine the horror of it. The same goes for child intimate abuse. We can only imagine the innocent suffering the child endures as their little body is violated. We all know what physical pain feels like, we know what fear, anger, and sadness feel like. So most of us, to some extent, can comprehend a horribly traumatic incident. We can and do react with compassion and support at the time of the incident. But the aftermath is a different story.

It is rare to hear any discussion relating to the emotional aftermath of these crimes, especially in the media, which is where we seem to glean most of our information. We may read a newspaper article about a specific intimate assault or child abuse case. We follow the story through, hopefully to a court trial with a just punishment. The same may go for the nightly television news reports. We learn, with concern, the disturbing facts about a case. We may pay attention until a legal outcome is reached, if there even is a legal outcome. Then we put it to rest. This seems to be as far as social comfort can go in its interest and understanding of the issue.

But the bigger picture is missed all together. A much bigger picture. Ask most survivors where their real pain lies, and they will tell you the actual physical assault or abuse was a walk in the park compared to the long-term emotional aftermath they have had to endure. This bigger picture is what needs to be known and understood if we are to create change in social attitudes. Would we be more willing to speak out, stop the silence, and set aside our discomfort if we knew more? Because once we know more, we can and must do more. Would we truly and decisively decree "no tolerance" for all intimate violence against any man, woman, or child? Would punishments finally fit the crimes?

Not long ago, I was watching a television episode of *The Practice*, a doctor/hospital TV drama series. This particular show was a rerun I had not seen. It dealt with the rape of the female chief of staff. Normally, I steer clear of television or movies that feel the need to display violence toward women or anyone else for that matter. (Yes, this definitely limits my movie-going experience). But I was compelled to watch this particular episode. I was interested in their portrayal of the intimate assault. I wondered if they were going to get it right.

The victim in this particular show was badly beaten as well as raped. She reported the physical assault to the police, but she did not report the intimate assault. She also told the police that her wallet had been stolen. She said nothing about the rape. She told no one. Her nose was broken, her right eye was bloody and swollen shut, her left wrist was fractured and in a cast, and the long cut on her right forearm required several sutures. As she lay in her hospital bed, a doctor came in and said he was going to give her something for the pain. He asked her where she was hurting the most. She told him, "my soul."

They got it right.

The long-term emotional aftermath is not easily understood by society. And understandably so, due in part to our silence. Often times, it is not even understood by the survivors themselves. During my many years of quiet watching, listening, and observing society, and still today, I believe there are those who continue to view intimate assault as just extremely rough, unsolicited sex, especially when the rape is not a "stranger in the bushes" case. Who knows, she was probably behaving foolishly and asking for it. After all, it was just sex gone bad. They think the physical wounds will heal, and she will quickly get over the upsetting incident. They are wrong. They are wrong because the pain has gone far beyond the physical and has settled deep within the heart and soul of the victim.

They don't know about the part that has taken me to the edge of sanity and left me there. Or how my very essence, my sacred, spiritual core has been found and mangled. It is deep within this soulful place, this place we all uniquely possess. It is this place that is ours alone, this place we protect so naturally. This is where my pain and sadness have settled.

It is from this soul pain that the residual effects will emerge and linger. Possibly for weeks, months, or even years. The complexity of emotions cannot be put to rest overnight, even though the disturbing incident is over and done with. It is a process. But the process is stifled by our silence.

I try not to think of my physical wounds. I ignore them, knowing they will mend. I know my body will soon heal and once again be strong. That is not where my pain is right now. It's something else. Something else is hurting so much worse than my body . . . My denial continues to have its way with me. I go to work and attend my classes as though nothing inside my soul has changed. I am determined that my life will not skip a beat. This almost-tangible ache in my spirit will go away. If I don't talk about it, it will go away. I can do this in my silence . . . Many weeks have passed, and the darkness is lingering, nagging. I don't want to be here. I want to go home . . . I drop my classes, I quit my job, and I make the long drive back home to my parents. Now I'll be okay. This is what I need. I will leave the darkness behind.

Most victims of intimate assault want their whole experience put behind them quickly. They don't want to think of it anymore. They have survived (they think) and want life to be as it once was. Those around the victim want the same. As they observe the victim functioning in some semblance of "life as usual," they can assume all is well and life goes on. But victims are very good at masking the pain and confusion that is being played out in the depth of their spirit. The mask can keep everyone's comfort level status quo. They mask to protect themselves, and they mask to protect those around them.

In my silence, I am stubbornly determined to beat back the darkness and pain surrounding my soul. I hang on tightly to the me I once knew. I will still be quick with a smile, and I won't scrimp on my laughter. I am embracing all the good blessings in my life, and I remain grateful, but something feels different . . . I am back in school, studying as before, but something feels different . . . I easily land a satisfying nursing position after graduation, but something feels different . . . I marry and am blessed with two beautiful baby girls, but something feels different . . . A handful of people close to me know my secret, but we never ever mention it. I know I am broken, but they don't. They can't see the cracks from the outside. Silence is all we know. And I am quick to understand the message of silence. I have learned over the years to be very careful with my mask. It is my armor that is supposed to protect me from the persistent sadness. It is supposed to help me forget that my beautiful, innocent spirit was crushed so suddenly. My mask is supposed to keep my denial in place and allow my spirit to be what it once was.

A survivor of intimate assault or intimate child abuse will inevitably experience a pervasive change that affects their spirit, soul, or very essence (call it what you will). What they once knew to be true of life has been replaced by a very different reality. It is a reality born of betrayal, humiliation, fear, mistrust, and pain. Their perception of self has been disturbed. The harsh loss of innocence can be played out in ways that will affect all aspects of one's life for years. The change was not a voluntary change. It was not a change the survivor asked for and the loss of who she or he once was can be profound. They will grieve for what was taken and wonder who and what they might have been if not for the residual effects of the trauma. They will wonder if they lived up to their potential or did the frequent distractions of pain, anger, and sadness get in the way. Did their feelings of diminished self-worth and self-respect hinder their aspirations? If the struggle to survive emotionally had not taken precedence over every day goals would they have been better equipped to be their best self?

My joy is indescribable as I sit for hours just taking in the beautiful sight of my new baby girl. She is barely a month old, and I have never felt such a love. I am in awe of this miracle of life, my miracle of life. I check her toes and tiny fingers for the hundredth time. How can skin be so perfectly pink and soft? She is happy. I can tell she is happy. Her dark blue eyes follow mine, and I know she is telling me I am her world. I am the one who will be her safe place. My tears start suddenly without warning. I can't stop crying. I am sobbing from deep within. The darkness is back. It has now followed me to my most important and cherished time of life. It has no business here. But it is here, and it questions me. Are you worthy enough to be the mother of this perfectly pure child? Can you be all that this precious little human being deserves? I cannot stop crying. I am less than. I am broken and can still feel that scar carved into my soul. My baby girl deserves the best, and I am not the best.

Those four guys left me with shadows of sadness and pain, and those shadows follow me, no matter which way I turn. Will I ever get used to it? Am I supposed to get used to it? Perhaps. I am still good at keeping my mask in place, but I do long for the me I used to be. The old me didn't feel less than and unworthy. The old me didn't feel damaged. The old me had never heard of PTSD, post-traumatic stress disorder, nor ever imagined the constant weight of an old, dark memory. The old me was not an anxious girl and was never claustrophobic. The old me wasn't bothered by loud, sudden noises or bright flashes of light. Maybe I'm not being fair in blaming all my peculiarities on my trauma. Maybe I would have been this way regardless. But I think not. I have a very good sense of who I am. I know my personality. I know where I came from. And none of these peculiarities jive with the me I know. Intellectually and emotionally I am out of sync. My emotions will not stay in tune with my intellect, even as my intellect attempts to reason with me. It is trying to convince me of all that I should know to be true. I am a good and decent woman. I am worthy and not less than. I am no different from any other beautiful soul. I am not broken. But my emotions are persuasive and win out over intellect. These emotions feel so foreign to me, and every one of them continues to stir up that dark place deep within my spirit.

As with any trauma one might experience, there is the emotional aftermath. Often a long-term emotional aftermath. It's not likely the soldier coming home from war can neatly tuck away all that he or she encountered on the battlefield. A parent who has lost a child will never "get over it." Victims of various serious crimes or accidents will not easily forget that frightening day. Tragically lost loved ones do not fade in memory. There is a healing process, and the healing comes in stages. It can be as time consuming and complicated as peeling an onion, one thin layer of skin at a time. Although the survivor can heal and become emotionally healthy once again, the expectation to "get over it" may never happen. They don't "get over it," but they can and do work "around it." They can put it in a place deep inside that allows them to maneuver their life around it. It does not have to get in the way of living a rich, rewarding life. It does not need to define who they are or what they are capable of accomplishing in their life.

Acceptance of one's trauma is essential in the healing process. Brushing the experience aside or attempting to deny it will only delay complete healing and recovery. Fully accepting the reality of one's rape, abuse, or any other trauma can now put us on top of it. We become in charge. It no longer has to be the weight that holds us down as we attempt to deny or disregard. It is what it is. Life happens. Experiences do not disappear. When we are able to achieve acceptance, we are then able to make the choices necessary to heal and take back control of our life.

It is important that we are able to accept the trauma as part of one's personal history, to put it in its place and regain the strength to move forward toward the life we choose to live.

But the healing is not likely with our silence, isolation, and denial, either as a society or as survivors. No matter what the traumatic experience, survivors heal best with compassion, support, and understanding. They heal best knowing their voice is heard, and they are not alone in their pain. The survivor must reach out and keep reaching out until he or she finds the support they need to put their broken pieces back together.

*   *   *

"We as victims/survivors lose a part of ourselves that we may never fully get back . . . It has been twenty-nine years since my rape and often throughout the years it seems as though the assault just happened yesterday. Everything seems to be going good in my life, and the next thing I know, something triggers the memories of the assault, and once again I feel like a prisoner in my own body: afraid of everything and everyone, always questioning other people's intentions toward me. I wonder if I will ever be able to trust again?"

Marissa
Intimate assault survivor

"On June 6, 1999, my whole world changed . . . How long am I going to live with self-doubt and self-hatred? How long until I'm whole again? That night ruined me. It broke me. It made me feel unworthy of happiness. It made me think that I was completely worthless and that nobody would ever love me . . . It made drugs the only things that could lift me out of that self-loathing. I found the one thing that could make the world perfect. Crystal meth. Oh, how it made me feel whole. It made the anger and the hate go away. It made the violence go away. The only time I felt free was when I was tweaking. There was no fear. Only pleasure. That was the first time I really enjoyed sex since my rape. I felt like I could climb mountains, jump rooftops, and save the world. I was unstoppable . . . It took me a little over a year to get off the drugs. It took me another couple months to leave my abusive boyfriend behind. I can't help but wonder if I had had more self-respect and had felt more self-worth would I have seen the red flags . . . I was robbed of everything I held dear and everything I took for granted. He stole my soul. He stole my self-respect. He stole my dignity. He stole my sense of safety. He stole everything and shit all over it."

Sarah
Intimate assault survivor

"I feel mentally destroyed. Anger, anxiety, and trust issues. It is clear to me that so much of this is because of what happened to me in my past. I don't trust men and find it hard to even have a normal relationship . . . My father and uncle have caused me pain that is still with me today. I don't hate my dad, but I do hate what he did to me and so many other children. Still today, when I think or speak of my dad, that soft spot in my heart makes me cry . . . My father is

doing sixteen years. I wonder if I will ever fully recover and
heal."

Tina
Child intimate abuse survivor

*"Rape strips you to your core. The physical attack will never
compare to the mental havoc."*

Dee
Intimate assault survivor

*"When I was seventeen, I left home. I was on my own in
Las Vegas, Nevada. I partied a lot. I survived for years
without any big problems. No one could hurt me because
I would never let anyone in . . . I married a guy when I
was twenty-one . . . We went to church . . . I could never be
as good as the other ladies. I felt different because I was
still broken. The depression was beyond anything I had ever
known. For years I cried, wouldn't eat, and slept for ten and
twelve hours at a time."*

Aly
Intimate assault survivor

*"The sexual and emotional abuse that took place in my early
childhood was profoundly life altering. Life altering enough
that as a young child, a chemical change took place in my
brain that was and still is irreversible without medications.
This was not determined until being diagnosed with
dysthymia and anxiety in my adulthood . . . The aftermath
of my abuse was profound and changed me for life. It made
my early childhood extremely painful and lonely. Looking
back at pictures from my childhood, I can see that I never
smiled. I used to think about Humpty Dumpty and changed
his name to mine."*

Anna Panna sat on a wall
Anna Panna had a great fall
All the king's horses and all the king's men
Couldn't put Anna Panna back together again.

Anna
Child intimate abuse survivor

"*As I think about my life, I can understand why I am the way I am now. I tend to hide myself away, barely going anywhere, tucking myself away from the world . . . I have trouble with anxiety . . . suffering from what I gather to be night terrors—horrible nightmares where I wake up crying and yelling . . . I wake up in panic attacks . . . I have a hard time getting to sleep, and then I have a hard time staying asleep. I'm tired all the time . . . I'm afraid most of the time. I can't live alone; when I do, I get almost no sleep, constantly waking up to check locks and such . . . and I never know what I'm afraid of or even why I'm so afraid.*"

Amy
Child intimate abuse survivor

When the court sentencing finally happened, I told the judge that the offender had given me a life sentence by committing this crime, so he should have a life sentence as well . . . It's been over six years since that night, and to say that my life has changed is an understatement . . . I spent a little time in counseling, mostly because a lot of people told me it would be a good idea, but I didn't think I needed it. I had convinced myself that I could get through this with little problem, and I felt that being a Christian meant that I wasn't going to let this get the best of me . . . I started having nightmares. One night, I dreamt that I was asleep in my house and someone broke in and was trying to hurt me. I did everything I could do to protect myself from being victimized again. I tried every self-defense technique I had learned since my attack. I shot him, I stabbed him, I did everything, and it still didn't stop him. I woke up feeling so defeated. I woke up thinking there really isn't anything I can do. I can be as prepared as possible, and this can still happen to me again . . . I have lived my life believing in God and having a personal relationship with him, but now I battle thoughts of how could my God have let this happen to me? What do I do with these feelings? Had he closed his eyes that night or for some reason looked away from me to allow me to be exposed to such evil? But at the same time, I knew that God hadn't left me completely because of how the events of that night unfolded . . . The beliefs and faith I had built my life on were crumbling, and I couldn't figure out how to get past it . . . I couldn't fight anymore, I didn't have anything left inside to fight for myself. I needed answers and tried everything to get some relief. My breaking point came quick . . . For the first time in my life, I could understand why some people are addicted to drugs. I had so much anxiety and unrest that I was willing to do just about anything to be able to escape. I was just so tired. I wanted to go to sleep and never wake up . . . I shared with my family how scared I was. They were scared for me and encouraged me to call a pastor friend of mine . . . I was hesitant to share with him that I was doing drugs to escape the pain and that I was more than doubting my faith. But knowing that I was honestly so close to ending my life, I felt that I had to at least try . . . I spilled everything, and to my relief, he didn't shake his head or tell me how horrible I was for trying to find relief anywhere and everywhere. For the first time, I heard someone tell me it was okay to have all the feelings I had been having. To be angry, hurt, sad, and so very scared, and it was even okay for me to feel these things toward God. He also proposed the idea that I needed to allow myself time to mourn. The person I was before I was assaulted is not the person I am now, and it was like losing a loved one. Not to say that I was somehow incomplete or damaged by any means but a different person. I was going through a process and needed to allow myself time to work through it . . . I still have plenty of moments when I grieve, and I allow myself those times. As more time passes, it seems the bad days are fewer, and I don't fight them anymore. There are times when I wonder how in the world I am making it through this, how am I going to sleep at night and not living in complete, petrifying fear? It's when those thoughts come up that I remind myself that I am doing this, and there is hope for a real life after your worst fear is forced upon you. It takes time. I still hold my breath when I walk into a dark room, and sometimes I just won't do it because I just can't, and I'm okay with that . . . The judge sentenced him to life in prison without parole."

Jaime
Intimate assault survivor

"The strange thing about being abused is that it stays with you wherever you go and with whomever you meet . . . it is a wound you carry . . . The trust between a child and parent is sacred. When that is violated, trust is hard to have for anyone. Any sense of trust I have for people has to be earned due to the fact that I never had a trustworthy bond with my parents. I raised myself and continue to parent myself on a daily basis."

Allecia
Child intimate abuse survivor

"When the rape happened I went into a dark shell. The world I went to was a place only God and I could be. I learned to find solace in my solo world. The outside world was no longer. The only reality was my inner world. I shut out the world altogether . . . You can forget the physical pain with time and try to get your life together. But the psychological damage is what I have had the most problem with . . . It's endless what the damage had done to my life. It's been a struggle for decades to try to get my inner self to match my outer self. My mind and intellect wanted to achieve so much. But my soul and my heart were so damaged, broken into a million pieces. I couldn't seem to make anything happen for myself. I couldn't blend my inner world with my outer world. I had such a lock on my soul that it acted as an anchor to everything in my life. It made me suicidal for years and years . . . I still battle self-doubt and am very, very self-conscious. I'm insecure about myself in close relationships. Trying to be more self-assured is a constant fight. Perhaps I will never get over it but I try . . . I haven't learned to trust men with my gift, the gift of me, my soul and my body. Don't know if I ever will."

A. G.

Intimate assault survivor, child intimate abuse survivor

"Out of all the events in my fifty-five years, my physical rape represents only minutes out of the entirety of my life. It was traumatic to say the least, but what was more traumatizing for me was not acknowledging what it did to me mentally, emotionally, and spiritually . . . I kept my secret. Did I not tell anyone because I felt I didn't matter? . . . It took me years to realize and acknowledge the devastation to my soul, that my soul had been fractured. The physical heals quickly, but how do I put my soul back together? This is

the journey I am on today, all these years later . . . Today I know we must tell. It is imperative to tell someone and not harbor the assault. Tell someone and keep telling until that someone listens. Tell."

Nanette
Intimate assault survivor

POEM UNTITLED

*S*omething so painful happened behind this home and
hearth.
*This place should not be beautiful while withered and torn
apart.*
See the ivy overgrown, wood-rotted window without its glue?
Something this painful shouldn't be made to last!
*Painful memories hidden, scared and trapped behind that
glass.*
*You see that nail there, it pierced my heart. I'd forgotten
that window. I fall apart!*
*That foundation under that house crumbles to pieces,
years too late.*
*If I had gotten out sooner, if he'd never come in! Horrible
place this is. Hearth and home.*
*I never found peace and harmony here. Only agony to an
always breaking heart.*
Enjoy your view of the window, look your fill.
*Feel free to come back my friends. But please rest assured I
never will!*

Cita
Intimate assault survivor

CHAPTER 6

Male Issue

I am trying to think of one male I know who has never had a mother. Just one. And darn it anyway, I just cannot think of one. Nor can I think of any male who has never had a sister, daughter, aunt, wife, girlfriend, grandmother, cousin, or other female who has been close to his heart. So this is where my confusion lies. If violence against women is happening far too often in our society—and we know it is—where is the voice of outrage from our good men? Why do so many men in our society side-step the issue and accept it as just a women's issue?

Intimate assault and abuse are not just women's issues. Not by a long shot. But for generations that has been the perception. We know the majority of intimate assault victims are female, therefore have we misguidedly handed the issue over to them to make noise and figure out how to better protect themselves? The role of activist and advocate for victims of this gender violence has been played out for years by females. Strong women, weary of the silence and victimization of their sisters, began taking action, and they continue to tirelessly do so today. Their outrage is slowly being heard. But if we are to truly prevent and stop the violence, this must also become a male issue. It is a social bruising that desperately needs the attention and the voice of decent men.

Very few perpetrators of intimate violence are not male. Yes, females can and do commit these horrific crimes, but the overwhelming evidence shows that males are hurting females. We also know that males are hurting other males, their victims young and old. Even though the number of female victims far outweighs the number of male victims, one would think there would be obvious reasons for intimate assault and abuse to also be male issues.

But we know the embarrassment and humiliation experienced by the male victim can be particularly difficult to address because of the emotional nature of their crime. Males are socialized to be strong and tough, never vulnerable. "Manly" ways are deeply ingrained from boyhood and beyond. Men are expected to be able to defend themselves and may fear judgment from others who have no understanding of these crimes. Sadly, they keep their pain buried deep in hopes that it becomes invisible and disappears. Yet, it does not disappear.

Perhaps we should rethink our notion of what it means to be a man in our society. We should acknowledge that a man's soul and spirit can be broken as easily as a woman's, and the pain can cut as deep. We should look at the tears in a man's eyes as evidence of a truth and not encourage the unhealthy facade of a mask. To "man up" should not mean to hold down the frightening and confusing emotions that come with trauma.

Intimate assault must become a male issue. It must become the concern of a man as well as a woman. Not simply because victims can also be men and boys, but because uniting our strengths as male and female will undoubtedly bring about an energy necessary to stop the violence.

We are wired to feel that sense of connection, that sense of community. There is no benefit to anyone as we tolerate and brush aside the issue of violence against women. The disrespect, degradation, and humiliation will ultimately seep into the collective body of society and slowly chip away at its integrity. What affects the female will ultimately affect the male. And vice versa. The experiences of our young boys and the experiences of our young girls will undoubtedly and eventually mesh as lives connect. The manner in which we are able to be there for each other can make the difference in creating a more healthy and safe society. Only if one happens to live life as the true and rare hermit living high in the mountains or deep in the back hills are we able to escape the darkness of society and even then, we might depend on the kindness of another to occasionally check on our well-being. It is not likely that many of us get through life without a personal connection to another.

So it makes no sense to me that a society as progressive and enlightened as we appear to be still cannot wholeheartedly accept the concept that the male voice and attention are needed to help end intimate violence.

I know it pains Paul to hear about my past. He truly loves me and doesn't want to accept that the woman he cherishes was hurt in a way no woman should ever be hurt. I sense his discomfort as he struggles to say or do the right thing. He is a good man who cannot relate to the evil in others. What is most comfortable for him is if I stay in my silence. I clearly sense him pulling down the shade that will block out all shadows of my rape. I love my husband, so I will protectively keep my silence. It is my distant past and we will leave it alone . . . I do not wake him in the middle of the night to comfort me as yet another nightmare harasses my sleep. And when feelings of sadness overwhelm me, I am careful to keep my tears in check until I am safely alone. He doesn't question damp, red eyes as I'm stepping out of my shower. On those darkest days that sneak up out of nowhere, I have my list of excuses to explain away my melancholy: tired, busy, PMS, stress, headache. It is best I keep my silence.

I am a female, not a male, so I want to be careful not to cross the line in assuming I know much of the male psyche. Dr. John Gray authored a book titled *Men Are From Mars, Women Are From Venus* (HarperCollins 1992) and I suppose that title says it all. And if I were to be completely honest here, which is exactly my goal, I will acknowledge that a woman who is enthusiastically encouraging, pleading, and attempting to sway a man to see an issue as his own, well, she may not get the result she is hoping for. It is just the nature of the game. But male speaking to male might make the positive difference. Another male may be far more qualified to deliver the message in a way that other males will receive and absorb information with better understanding. It simply makes sense. Men understand men. The last thing we want is for a male to feel the need to position his defenses strategically around him, thus preventing these issues from getting his much-needed attention. Good men must understand that even though they or other men in their social circle would never consider hurting a woman, this issue does concern them.

Although female activists and advocates have been on the frontline of this fight against intimate violence from the beginning, it seems that more and more good, decent men are stepping up. They are passionate about taking on the fight as their own. These males are bravely using their voice to end gender violence. I say bravely because they are crossing barriers that have been in place for generations. They are saying it like it is and debunking the "boys will be boys" or "good 'ole boys" mentality. Nothing gives me more hope than hearing a man take the challenge and speak up.

Jackson Katz and Russell Strand are two such men.

Jackson Katz is a well-known anti-violence activist also working toward the prevention of gender violence. He is an educator, national speaker, and author. His book, *The Macho Paradox: Why Some Men Hurt Women and How All Men Can Help* (Sourcebooks 2006), is definitely worth the read. His educational video, *Tough Guise: Violence, Media, and the Crisis in Masculinity* (1999), brings to light the necessity for social change in our definition of manhood. We seem to have blurred the line between the good strength in a man and the destructive strength in a man.

Russell Strand is currently chief of the US Army Military Police School, Family Advocacy Law Enforcement Training Division. He speaks nationally and is a US Army and Department of Defense subject matter expert and consultant in the area of spouse and child abuse and intimate violence. He educates and speaks as an advocate for those traumatized by intimate violence. He does not mince words. His speeches are insightful and eye-opening.

Jackson Katz and Russell Strand get it. As do many other men who are now realizing that the time has come for men to step up. We are definitely on the right track but still not where we must be. Much more needs to be done as we continue to encourage men to take up the cause.

My silence is working for no one. I am sorry for Paul. I never intended to share my deepest and darkest and most personal sadness with him. I never intended to burden him with my pain and for it to become his own. I had no idea that the memories of that night so many years ago would still weave in and out of my world today. I know now that I cannot be alone with the pain . . . We tiptoe around the conversations. I try to share my thoughts with my husband, knowing I am not choosing the right words. It is difficult for me to find the proper language that will articulate my complicated emotions . . . I am reading some literature on intimate assault and the long-term effects it can have on its victims. I am identifying with almost every written word on the pages of the booklet. This will make much more sense to Paul than my far-from-adequate attempt to explain my feelings. I ask Paul if he would be willing to read the booklet. He says, "Sure, Hon, set it on my nightstand and I'll read it." One week passes, and the booklet has not been touched. Two weeks pass, and it hasn't been touched. A month later, I quietly take the untouched booklet from his nightstand and put it away. I am once again alone in my pain . . . Paul will be the first to tell you he did not want to acknowledge the rape of his wife. He will tell you he could not acknowledge anything that would blemish the pureness and innocence of his wife, his soul mate. He sees me as goodness, and the ugliness of my rape was a place he could not go. That I was hurt in such a way is a pain he wanted to deny. My rape did not fit into our relationship, spiritually, physically, or emotionally. He wanted to protect our special place in this world by not letting it come near. I, more than anyone, could understand these feelings. He says he wanted to fix it but knew he could not. His silence was his way to calm his frustration. He wants a justice for me now that can never be.

We need men to be courageous enough to challenge other men's behavior: family, friends, coworkers, business associates. I am not talking about the "put up your dukes" kind of challenge. The challenge of conversation can work just fine. Okay, okay, I know we're talking male here. So let us just say a conversation of few words—effective enough. The days of acceptance and tolerance of bad behavior must end. We can no longer afford to continue ignoring destructive words and behavior. The discomfort of stepping up is a small price to pay. We have paid a far bigger price for our silence.

Silently shrugging off the brutish, tough guy remarks of others only serves as a pass for the offender to continue his behavior. He has not been challenged. He has not been made to stop and rethink his words and actions.

If a man is witnessing the disrespect or mistreatment of a woman, man, or child he must speak up. He must make it his business, because it is not okay to look the other way.

The young man out partying with his friends may be doing his drunken buddy a huge favor by steering his intoxicated friend (potential rapist, harsh but accurate) away from the young woman who is not interested in being forced into anything. So not only is the woman being indirectly looked after but also a potential criminal lawsuit has been averted. That is the kind of friend you want.

How we influence the behavior of our young boys plays a significant role in how the lives of our big boys unfold. Role-modeling makes all the difference. Little boys are paying close attention to the big men in their lives. They want to be like them when they grow up. It is not enough that we speak the "do as I say, not as I do" platitude. They are watching our behavior more than listening to our words. Eventually, the watching turns into mimicking. If dad is disrespectful to women, you can bet that little boy will do the same. And it breaks my heart to know that little boy was born with the potential to be molded into a man of decent character and principles. He was not born disrespectful. He was taught.

We must be mindful of the kind of role models we are to our young boys. We must teach our little boys that disrespect to any male or female is unacceptable. And our behavior must reflect that. We must teach our little boys that the physical strength of a man is not used to hurt others. And our behavior must reflect that. We must acknowledge that males are born with the same human emotions of fear, sadness, anger, and joy that females are born with, and males must be allowed to express those feelings without being looked upon as "unmanly." The little boy who is told to "stop crying like a baby" is one step closer to growing into a man with an unhealthy suppression of emotions. He will be socialized to believe that this is what it means to be a real man. On the contrary, it is a courageous and genuine man who is able to engage his emotions and deal with them accordingly. Proper and decent role-modeling for our young boys will have a significantly positive effect in the prevention of gender violence.

Prevention is the key to this issue of gender violence. After the fact is too late. Yes, we can offer support, compassion, resources, and legal services once the violence is played out, but a spirit has yet again been broken and forever changed. We can continue to keep the focus on females, telling them what they need to do to keep themselves safe. We have lots of "dos and don'ts" when it comes to being a female. Everything from what she should and should not wear to where she can and cannot go. How she must guard her drink as though it was the most valuable piece of property she owns to taking on a most uncomfortable hypervigilance once the sun goes down. These scenarios are routinely familiar to females. But focusing on what a female needs to do *not* to be the victim of a crime hardly seems to be the solution.

Prevention must be the focus. And males, along with females, must take on the challenge.

My healing came and continues to come in baby steps—as did the awareness, understanding, and support of my husband. At the risk of sounding completely corny, I can tell you that today my husband is my hero. We talk often and openly about the reality of intimate assault and the effects it has had on us as a man and woman. Paul now knows that speaking out as a man is essential to a society in need of changing its attitudes regarding intimate violence. He knows this social issue is not only a woman's issue but an issue men need to address as they help carry the burden of change. He actively does his part in the community to make this difference. I am not on my own anymore. Paul knows my spirit and all its scars, and he is as careful as he can be with them. And for this I love him with all my heart.

There is no way to sugarcoat it. Males are hurting females. It is time this senseless behavior stops. Good, strong, and decent men are capable of influencing other good, strong, and decent men. They are capable of ensuring that our young boys will grow up with a respect for males and females alike. Making this a male issue can make a difference. Men and women working together will make the difference.

*   *   *

"Humans are being victimized. Abusing other human beings. Gender does not nor should not matter. Communities are beginning to recognize this—that this issue is about anybody and everybody. Males are beginning to speak out . . . Our society is so mired in violence and war. Religious sex scandals. Our collective conscience is becoming weary. We are hearing more. It is seeping out the edges and through the barrier chinks. Slowly more and more are stepping forward to speak out. This is good. This is the beginning of healing. To break from that self-doubt and shame, that's got to be positive.

I can tell by their hug as we say good-bye . . . I have sat with them through their forensic SART (Sexual Assault Response Team) *exam knowing they were angry and extremely hurt. They are male and they are female. They are angry at having to be there, period. Not because of me, not because of my gender . . . They hug me good-bye; it's a big hug, and it's always a hug of gratitude. Because they knew they were respected in my presence."*

Ben
Advocate for victims of intimate assault

"One of the males in my family, along with a male friend of mine, wanted to find the guy who had hurt me. Their plan was to take a baseball bat to him and hurt him. I remember telling them that they would only end up in jail. Instead they decided to use the baseball bat to bust out the windows of the rapist's truck."

Marissa
Intimate assault survivor

"I was attending a workshop on healing. As I was sharing my story with the men and women in my group, I was shocked by the reactions of the males in the group. I was dumbfounded by their anger and initially thought it was directed toward me. But their anger was not directed at me. They were actually more in tune with what had happened to me than I was myself. Their anger was directed toward the behavior of those boys who had hurt me. As good, kind, and decent men, they were outraged at the behavior of men who hurt women, and their anger was in response to my story. They felt the mistreatment of women by some men reflected back on to those good men who did not hurt women. They felt the bad behavior of some men affects and hurts those men who choose to be kind and loving in their relationships. Their anger was in response to my story and how I was mistreated. That's what they were angry about, and that's what they wanted me to know."

Nanette
Intimate assault survivor

"It's challenging to know most sexual assaults are committed by males. Of course, all males do not assault, but more male involvement would help show that there are many males who personally or morally feel they can help when help is needed

the most. As a male advocate for victims of sexual assault, I can hope to do my small part in making this a male issue, an issue that concerns all . . . I am a male advocate, but more importantly, I am simply one person wanting to help another person. If the survivors can look at this with that same perspective, I feel I can be of help to them when they are in need of emotional support . . . My two sons, twenty-one and twenty-five, have been very supportive of my work. My male coworkers remark positively and feel it's noble to take interest in this issue. One particular coworker now volunteers at the crisis center after hearing of my involvement . . . This is not just a female issue."

Bill
Advocate for victims of intimate assault

"Our society only worsens the situation by framing it as a women's issue. How backward are we to see men committing these horrible acts and somehow decide this is not a male problem? It is because of this glaring hypocrisy that it cannot be understated how important it is for good and honorable men to join the fight and take a stand against this behavior. The philosopher Edmund Burke is attributed as saying, 'All that is necessary for the triumph of evil is that good men do nothing' . . . A great plague for years has been brought against the women that we love, gentlemen. We should be ashamed by our inaction . . . Perhaps nothing would better alleviate your personal rage than to rise up violently against these criminals, a sort of vigilante justice, but it will not solve the problem and would only continue the chain of violence. No, it is prevention and damage mitigation that fall to us. We can foster a social environment that will not tolerate sexually violent joking or playing. We can teach our sons to respect all people and to never act out

any sexual behavior without the express permission of their partners. We can tell our friends that the sexually violent joke wasn't funny and encourage them to think about the consequences of what they are saying. Most importantly, we must pay attention to our surroundings. For the sake of our wives and girlfriends, our daughters and granddaughters, our friends and colleagues. If we see any signs of sexual assault, we must intervene. Call the police immediately or alert security. If capable, we ourselves can intervene until help arrives . . . And when the unthinkable happens, we must mitigate the damage as best we can. Above all, be supportive of the survivor in your life. They do not need a warrior, which might be our first instinct. They need a gentle voice and the reassurance that we love them. This was not their fault . . . It's a very small percentage of men who feel so entitled to commit these acts. The majority of men are law-abiding and decent. But our loved ones can no longer afford for us to be a silent majority. We must stand up and do something so that evil will not prevail. And if we refuse, if we cannot take it upon ourselves to stand up for this most basic freedom, the autonomy of each person's body, then we become as guilty as the perpetrator for allowing this to continue. We are better than that. We must be better than that."

Brandon
Law enforcement advocate for victims of intimate assault

CHAPTER 7

Forgiveness

Forgiveness is a glorious gift we give ourselves. At a quick glance we might think the gift is intended for another. The offender. It is not. But are we not forgiving the offender for the harm he or she has done to us? Are we not telling the bad guy we are no longer hurt, offended, or affected by his destructive deeds and all is well? Not at all. Forgiveness is not about the bad guy. It is not about letting him off the hook for the pain he has delivered to another. Forgiveness is about freeing one's self from the oppressive and painfully heavy burden we carry with us when we have been wronged.

Forgiveness does not mean forgetting. Forgiveness does not mean accountability and responsibility are set aside. Or that justice can be neglected. Survivors of many different crimes have forgiven their perpetrators as those perpetrators sit day after day in their prison cells. Forgiveness dismisses nothing. The offender is where he needs to be. But survivors who have yet to explore forgiveness may often be in their own undeserved prison cell.

Forgiveness can release us from our emotional prison. It rarely comes without a personally intense internal struggle, especially with the most serious offenses. It is a hard-fought battle as we attempt to reach that place of forgiveness. I believe in the goodness of forgiveness, but I also absolutely respect the notion that there are those who simply cannot bring themselves to forgive the detestable actions of others. That is their right and their choice.

For twenty years I have wished them dead. For twenty years I have wanted them to know my pain. These thoughts do not come from a place of anger; I wish they did. The anger would be healthier, perhaps goading more of the fight in me. But it's the sadness that has always consumed me and has left little room for my right to a justified anger. I simply want them to know my pain and loss because it is only fair . . . I can't stop crying today. It's one of those days, and I'm feeling so sad, dark, and alone. I hurt so bad I think I can feel the broken pieces of my spirit. I think of the girl I was back then, and I am so sorry for her. I am crying for her and all that she lost. I want them to feel her pain. I want them to hurt like she hurts.

Feelings of anger, sadness, and pain are legitimate and justified emotions we experience when we have been the victim of someone's wrongdoing. Thoughts of revenge are even understandable, although a vindictive spirit would most likely delay and interfere with the positive energy necessary to begin the healing process.

It is not always possible or even necessary to be face to face with the one who has harmed us in order to forgive. The desire to forgive does not always come quickly to us. And when we are finally ready to rid ourselves of the painful hold our offender has on us, circumstances may have changed. Time and space may separate victim and offender. Or it simply may continue to be too painful for a survivor to be physically anywhere near the offender.

It is not necessary to look into the eyes of the bad guy in order to forgive him. It is not necessary for you to see his face or for him to hear your words. Because this forgiveness is ultimately for the one who has been harmed. This forgiveness is to free us from the intrusive, all-consuming thoughts swirling around in our heads that prevent us from abandoning the shadow of the offender. Forgiveness can release us from those dark emotions that get in the way of our path to healing. The constant distraction of having a specific target (our offender) simply keeps feeding our anger, pain, and frustration.

It is very likely that those who have caused such pain and turmoil in another's life have gone on with their lives, oblivious to the long-term emotional struggle the victim is left to deal with. The offender may have little concern or maybe has forgotten all together that the harm they did to another has left its mark. It serves no good purpose to hold on to angry thoughts directed toward the offender when they themselves are so unaware of the ongoing grief they have created. We are only hurting ourselves, we are not hurting them, which is reason to understand that forgiveness is as much for those harmed as it is for those who have harmed.

The thought that I could forgive those four guys never occurred to me until now, thirty-three years later. I'm not a vengeful person; I'm not an angry person. So why have I not thought of forgiveness before now?

It's curious to me that for most of the years since the rape I have had no memory of those four faces and only one had a name, which I knew back then. For years now, even that name slips from my memory, a name I cannot be sure of. Very early on those faces blurred together, thankfully preventing my mind from clearly seeing more than I need to see. Too much of that night has already been indelibly etched into my brain. I don't need or want to remember faces. They could pass me on the street today, look me in the eye, and I wouldn't know them. This seems odd to me, because I had plenty of time to see their faces that horrible night. But seeing no faces has not removed the disturbing image of four young men hurting one young woman. Seeing no faces has not kept them from haunting me whenever they choose.

Paul and I are attending a spiritual weekend retreat in a tiny California town. I love this place, tucked away between mountains, forest, and farmlands. It gives me the serenity and solitude I crave . . . Father Tom is talking about forgiveness and suggests a spiritual exercise for all of us. He wants everyone to reflect on the idea of forgiveness and then write a letter of forgiveness to whomever we choose. This letter of forgiveness can be written to ourselves, or the letter can be written to forgive another. It is our own private letter that we will then fold up and one by one we will toss into the burning fire pit outside. We can forgive and let go of the painful hold another has had on us. It is not until I listen to Father Tom's words that I consider the peace forgiveness might bring me. I need this. I can do this. After all these years, I am ready for something, anything, to dim the pain. I can forgive those four guys . . . I get out my paper and pencil, ready to start my letter. But the words are not there. Nothing is coming to me. Come on, just write. I need to do this. But my sadness overwhelms me and the tears begin. I am back in my paralyzing pain. Written words are not coming to me, only the frightening images of four. I get up, quietly walking out of the room to be alone with my sadness—alone to cry until my tears eventually calm me. Before returning to my group, I encounter Jane and Chris, two genuinely beautiful, compassionate women who are Father Tom's retreat assistants. I tell them I cannot write the letter. I feel foolish and embarrassed. They don't question me but lovingly tell me to simply fold up my blank piece of paper and throw it into the fire as we all complete the exercise of forgiveness and release. No one has to know my paper is blank . . . Paul and I are making the hour-long drive home from the retreat. Driving through the beautifully serene Sierra Valley we are silent, both lost in our own personal reflections. I feel bittersweet. The retreat has rejuvenated me spiritually, which gives me what I need to continue bringing hope, strength, and joy into my life. At the same time, I am feeling so disappointed in myself for not reaching that place of forgiveness that I needed to achieve. I should have been able to write that letter. Instead, I had felt weak and bullied by memories. So I begin my conversation with my higher power, who I refer to as God. We talk, or I do anyway. I'm letting Him know I have the desire to forgive, and I am asking Him for help. I want the forgiveness to be sincere and authentic, not just empty words I speak in hopes they do the trick. I'm asking Him to help me figure out a way

I can go about forgiving four young men with faces I cannot see, with names I do not know. I only know that their shadows have haunted my spirit and my soul for far too many years. I want my thoughts to lead me to a positive place. I begin to realize and to know that each of these faceless men came into this life as somebody's precious, beautiful baby boy. I begin to see them as innocents, who began their lives with perfect little souls, worthy of all the love, nurturing, and protection every other little baby boy deserves. I see them as God's creation. I can only think something must have gone terribly wrong in their own lives for them to become who they are and for them to make the choice to hurt another human being. Their actions are detestable, their souls are not. I am slowly feeling lighter as though something or someone is peeling away dark heavy shadows that have surrounded me and weighed me down for more than thirty years. I have forgiven. And I am feeling the freedom of true forgiveness. Physically and emotionally . . . I was an insignificant young woman to those four young men, and over the years, I doubt they have given me a second thought. They certainly will not ever know that I have forgiven them. And that is fine with me. Because the gift of forgiveness is mine. I did it for me. I can feel it, and I am grateful.

I am no longer concerned with my rapists. I have no space in my head for them now and have dismissed them from my life. I am free of their oppressive images and thoughts of them at this very moment stir no emotions within me. Forgiveness is allowing me to move on to continued healing. I believe in Karma, and I believe in God. At this point, I will leave the business of payback to Him.

Forgiveness can bring us closer to living in that most desirable place of "now." The place of this moment. If we are truly living in the moment, right "now," we are able to leave the sorrow of the past behind. We cannot undo the past; we cannot change the experiences we have endured. But that is our history; it is not our present. Forgiveness clears away those cluttered thoughts of people in our past who have done us harm and makes room for positive, purposeful energy to make "now" the best it can be.

"Now" can allow gratitude to fill our moments and release the angst of yesterday and uncertainty of tomorrow. What is past is past, it is a done deal, and there is no going back. And as much as we would like to believe we have control over our tomorrows, we simply do not. Of course, we have our dreams and goals that we are hopeful our future brings to us. These dreams and goals make life worthwhile and give meaning to our days. But what truly matters is how we are making the most of "now." We have choices in how we live and appreciate "now." Each moment is a new beginning. If and when we stray from living in the moment (and no doubt our humanness will cause us to stray), the past can slyly work its way back into our consciousness. It can pull us into a place that serves no good purpose, as does the unproductive worry and anxiety of what our future might bring. Living in the present is the most freeing place to be. We make the most of "now" by freeing ourselves from an obstructive past and avoiding the unnecessary and useless dread and worry of tomorrow. Live one day at a time, one hour at a time, and if we must, one minute at a time.

Forgiveness releases us from the burdensome and undeserving hold of another. It makes way for a more focused path to healing. It brings us a step closer to that joyous place of freedom: that time and place of "now."

*   *   *

"Forgiveness? I don't know if I've ever thought about it. But being the kind of person I am, I always try to find the good in people. I guess I do have some forgiveness for him. But I will not ever forget what he did to me."

Marissa
Intimate assault survivor

"As I've gotten a little older and a little wiser, I've learned to forgive. I forgave the man who raped me. I didn't forgive him for him. I forgave him for me. The anger and the hatred were killing me. He robbed me of everything once, and I was not going to let him control another second of my life."

Sarah
Intimate assault survivor

"Then there was my uncle. Not enough I had endured the pain of my father. I know it seems selfish for not turning him in, and I do apologize, but I was way too scared. His father was some bigwig in a small town. Lots of money. I didn't even want to think about what would have happened to me if I would have reported him. I won't give names. I figure God will handle him. I watched him hurt and take advantage of so many people, especially me. I know when he dies I will spit on his grave."

Tina
Child intimate abuse survivor

"Later in life, when I was probably around forty years old, I came to a place of forgiveness. After a few years of counseling, I reached that place that many sexual abuse victims reach when

*you say to yourself, 'I forgive him, but I will never forget.' . . .
It wasn't something that came overnight. It was something that
slowly evolved. As my step-dad got older and more frail, it was
easier to forgive. He died at age ninety-two, and I had taken
care of him in the last months of his life. That went well, and I
think he appreciated my help. But as awful as this may sound,
my true peace came after he died. That's when I felt it was all
over. That's when I really felt free. I still wear the scars, but I'm
at a place of acceptance and peace."*

Anna
Child intimate abuse survivor

*"A good friend of mine said it best when she told me
forgiveness is the process of letting go. And I have been
going through this process for a long time. I choose not
to let him victimize me any further. I choose to keep the
control rather than let him have any more control of me,
my life, or my future. As I work on letting go, I maintain
control. As difficult as it is, it is worth it. It doesn't change
what has happened to me or lessen the pain, but it does
allow me to have a choice. The control. Letting go is very
empowering."*

Jaime
Intimate assault survivor

*"Father and Mother are not words that are dear to me . . .
I often look at greeting cards and sometimes happen upon
Mother's Day cards. Nothing in those cards remotely says
how I feel about my mother or father. A good greeting for me
would say, 'You raped me when I was eight, would you mind
paying my twenty-year therapy bill?' My sense of humor
has kept me alive . . . I fight every day to work through the
pain of what I have lived through. I have days in which I*

feel that the evil that was done to me is unforgivable and unjust in so many ways. I come upon no words for the loss I have experienced. Some days the only thing I can do is be alive and spend time with my dogs, cats, or boyfriend. The rage is incredible . . . that's when I write songs, cry, or just go to sleep."

Allecia
Child intimate abuse survivor

"I am a very spiritual person, and I knew my healing had to be spiritual. Through the process, I began to realize the true depth of our spiritual capabilities. I believe we have power in the spirit and everything in the physical has to first come from the spiritual plane. If I was going to heal anything in the physical, be it my body, my heart, my mind, or my circumstances, I had to start from the spiritual . . . I don't condemn to hell the two men who abused me in my life. Although they made my life a living death every day, I let God deal with them. I hold no grudges. In doing so, I would only condemn myself to hell."

A. G.
Intimate assault survivor, child intimate abuse survivor

"It happened so many years ago, and I've come to believe that it's less about forgiving the three guys and more about forgiving myself for not doing something prior to the rape. He had threatened me so many times before the physical assault, and every time he would say, 'I'm going to get you.' I shoved my feelings down and swallowed them. His words were so threatening to me, I felt emotionally and spiritually assaulted even before the physical rape. I was very fearful of him with every threat . . . I have forgiven myself for not

doing something about his threats. I have forgiven myself for not listening to me. I was young and naive back then. I felt I didn't have any power over his threats. I didn't think anyone would take my words seriously. I was afraid my fears would be minimized by others . . . If someone is constantly telling you what he is going to do to you, you need to tell someone. Had I known how to respond to a threat, instead of just reacting in fear, I would have realized I needed to tell someone. Today, when someone tells me they are going to do something, I take them at face value and I act."

Nanette
Intimate assault survivor

Mary Ann Ricciardi, Mindy Hsu, Nicole Schauwecker,
Erica Jones, Ida Seiferd, 2011

Sheila Lynette Barrett
November 05-1947 to April 10-2009

CHAPTER 8

Support and Survival

*T*he human spirit is resilient, amazingly resilient. I have always been intrigued by this spirit strength we all possess. As a young girl, I was drawn to biographical stories of determination, inner strength, and survival. I chose book after book that inspired me and revealed to me the most remarkable traits of mankind. Still today, my bookshelves are filled with writings that continue to inspire hope, making known to me the extraordinary ability of human endurance.

Transitioning from victim to survivor is always possible; it is just not easy and does not necessarily happen overnight. No matter the trauma, it takes time. For some, the transition may take weeks or months, for others, years.

I am growing weary. My mask is slipping. I want to be done with these two separate but tightly parallel paths I have traveled for thirty years. One path has led me to a joyful, abundant, and grateful life. I have been blessed with the cherished love of parents, brothers, and sisters I adore. To this day, they fill my life with strength and love. They are my safe place. I have had the miraculous experience of being a mother to two beautiful daughters and the auntie to several adored nieces and nephews. I have a husband whose love I never doubt. And the remarkable friends I have gathered along the way are precious gifts I will never take for granted. But there is the other path, the dark path. It is my silent path that persistently reminds me of the pain and sadness deep inside my spirit. It is a lonely, isolating, and limiting path that leads me nowhere . . . I foolishly thought I could do this on my own. I thought I had to do this on my own. But thirty years later, I acknowledge I have done a pitiful job of mending myself. Life has a way of slowly creeping along, or so it seems. It is easy to become settled in our pain and darkness. But the reality is, life does not creep, it flies. And precious opportunities for a contented life are wasted. I realize now that my silence is holding me still, paralyzing me. It has kept my healing just beyond my reach, hovering in the distance. It is clear my silence has kept me in victim mode, rarely feeling the strength or courage of a survivor . . . I am ready to travel only one path.

There has been a push to encourage advocates for victims of intimate assault to speak of or speak to a new victim as "survivor." This, understandably, is to focus on the individual's positive recovery and return to self-empowerment. A survivor can take back control of her life and move forward. She can heal in a timely manner and regain her personal strength. But there are many variables that play a part in the ability to heal and survive. The outcome of a traumatic event can be influenced by a victim's age, background, and personality. The duration of abuse and the level of violence the victim has experienced can also affect the timetable of recovery. Most importantly, the positive support and compassion a victim receives or does not receive from those around her will undoubtedly be a factor in her recovery. The past silences from victims and society have proven to be detrimental in the healing process. There is no healing in the isolation and the silence. It is this support and compassion that are significant and can be the caring acts that nudge the victim to embrace the role of survivor in a timely manner.

That being said, I do have somewhat of a different take on the victim versus survivor label, and I am guessing my view is not a popular view. But still, I believe it is worth addressing.

I, more than anyone, wish to know the victim has eventually transitioned to survivor. And as quickly as possible. But to refer to a victim as a survivor very early on seems misleading—to society and to the victims. Simply because a victim has escaped, run, or walked away, still breathing, from the assault or abuse does not mean that she has survived. If we are merely talking in the physical sense, then yes, she has survived. Physically. But we now know that physical injuries are rarely the source of one's deepest pain or the ongoing struggles that follow intimate assault and abuse. It is the emotional and spiritual trauma that cut deeper. To suggest that one has immediately survived an assault and is now a survivor, in my opinion, minimizes the fact that this person was indeed the victim of a very serious crime. The definition of a victim is a person who suffers from a destructive or injurious action. For a time, many victims' souls have been gravely injured and their spirits have been destroyed. The reality is, she is a victim.

Survivor sounds much better than victim. More positive. More empowering. I get it. We want the victim to grab back control of her life and not let the offender have one more second of her time. In my experience as an advocate, I speak to victims throughout the six months after their assault, but not many speak as though they have survived emotionally. They are depressed, angry, frustrated, and unable to concentrate, and they continue fighting off nightmares. They are working in the direction of recovery and taking on the challenge to become a survivor, but simply labeling a victim "survivor" does not make it real.

My concern is that society in general will hear "survivor" and assume all is well. The survivor is back to normal and life is as it once was. She has survived. No need for concern. And this is exactly where society has plopped itself for generations: little concern because all looks and sounds well—oblivious to the long-term emotional aftermath a victim is left to deal with. Society does not need any more reasons to bury its head in the sand. The reality, although harsh, is that the victim was traumatized and will rarely bounce right back to the emotional health of a survivor. This takes time, and as uncomfortable as it may be for those surrounding the victim, we must, as a society, begin to pay attention to the emotional effects of these crimes. We must be patient.

I also wonder if we are doing the victim a favor if we refer to her as a survivor when she does not yet feel the strength of a survivor. Will she feel as though she should be stronger and in control of her life when she does not yet feel this way? Will she feel disappointed in herself and wonder why she is not recovering at the pace others feel she should be recovering? Will she bury her emotions deep down in order to appear to fit the survivor role? At some point in her life, these buried emotions will reappear and put her right back into victim mode. Perhaps it is the victim who knows best when she is a survivor, and she will take on that role as she herself makes that transition. We can make it our role to support her with compassion, listen without judgment, and encourage a return to self-empowerment. In doing so we are guiding her to know and believe in herself as a survivor. But this takes time, and we must be patient as the survivor emerges.

So much time has passed. I should be feeling better. Time should be helping me heal. But I am not feeling better. I am feeling worse. The PTSD is returning more often and for longer periods of time. I'm crying unexpectedly, and my concentration is minimal. The thirty years of recurrent nightmares are wearing me out. Everything is wearing me out. I want to be done . . . Who do I turn to? I am so used to being alone with this, but I know I cannot do it anymore. I am tired of the mask. I no longer care . . . Although I am surrounded by wonderful family and friends, I am embarrassed to reach out for help. I have waited thirty years to speak out and admit I need help. I am ashamed to admit I have not had the strength to fix myself as I once thought I could. I feel weak and hopeless . . . I am well aware of society's continued discomfort and lack of understanding regarding intimate assault. I see the tolerance; I hear the comments. I am not entrusting myself to anyone . . . I feel desperate today, scared for myself. I look in the phone book under "crisis," hoping to find a resource that will direct me to some kind of help. There is a number for a local crisis center that I did not even know existed. I am embarrassed to make this call, but I dial the number. I feel embarrassed and weak because I am telling this stranger I was raped thirty years ago, and I'm not doing very well. Will she exclaim that thirty years is quite a long time to wait before getting help? Aren't I over it yet? But that was not her response. The kind voice on the other end of the phone is not at all surprised, and she immediately and simply gives me a number for a support group that could possibly help me. I hang up the phone and dial the number.

I love to imagine, in my dreamlike state of mind, a world where there is no gender violence. A world with no rape, no child abuse, no human harming human. But I am no longer naive, and forgive my negative tone, but it is highly unlikely we will ever get to that perfect place. Human beings are imperfect. We will continue to do bad things. Believe me; I would so love for someone to prove me wrong. But knowing life will never be perfect must not stop us from doing whatever we can to make this world the best it can be for ourselves and for each other.

A world without rape is an ideal and worthy goal. Many are continuously and tirelessly working in that direction. But until we reach that better place, we can and must pay attention to how we are tending to the victims/survivors today. Victims will not embrace their survivor strength without the help of those around them.

Remaining a victim slowly crumbles the wholeness of self, family, community, and society. All are affected when we are not there for each other. It is time we become educated and set aside our misconceptions and discomfort to better understand the reality of these traumas. Simply turning away because we do not understand does not make the issue go away or make it nonexistent—it is only a detriment to us all.

I am filled with such anxiety as I drive myself to this support group. It is hard to breathe, and I am not trusting my stomach right now. Are they going to want me to speak? Am I going to have to go back to that dark and sad place? But I know that that is a silly thought, because I have been in and out of that darkness and sadness for thirty years. What difference does it make? Maybe now I will not be alone as I go there . . . This is the group? Three of us? It's okay. I feel safer with less . . . Misty introduces herself and the others. I cannot help feeling hopeful. We begin the session. I am crying with relief. I am speaking and they know. They know what has been caught deep down in my soul all these years. They are there for me because they know. I am there for them because I know . . . Misty is gentle, compassionate, and understands far more about me than I do myself. She is validating all those emotions I had stuffed deep down inside myself. All those emotions are coming to the surface, and the tears are coming with them. She is making sense of things I could not clearly see. She is guiding me toward that healing place. I am finding my voice, and the more I hear my voice, the more I feel my courage and power as a woman return to their rightful place. I am feeling a freedom and strength that have been long overdue. I can feel the huge breaks in my spirit slowly mending.

To be there for each other does not mean having to fix another's problem. Perhaps that imagined burden of thinking we have to fix someone's problem and not knowing how to do that is what keeps people from being there for each other during their most difficult times. It is not even necessary to fully understand what that person is going through in order to be there. Oftentimes, we just cannot understand another's pain. But that should never keep us from simply being there. And it is that simple. We can listen. We can comfort with a heartfelt hug. We can be open to the beginning of better understanding. It is really not that complicated.

The simplicity of just being there for another is often the most healing and most needed gesture we can offer a victim. This is the support that will encourage the victim to know and believe she is a survivor. The struggle to regain her personal strength is far easier when she realizes she is not alone in her pain. Professional support is also often necessary and encouraged. The sooner the victim is cared for, the sooner she becomes the survivor.

I am learning that the healing process is like peeling an onion. There are several fine layers in this long process. Just when I feel my healing is close to complete, I discover yet another layer of pain waiting to be dealt with. But I get it now, and I am patient with myself. It takes time . . . Life is what it is, and I cannot wish it away. I have learned acceptance. I had fought long and hard to prevent this ugly experience from laying claim to a place in my life and that impossible fight only weighed me down. I now understand there is no healing without acceptance. Like it or not, my rape experience has found its place within me, and it fits. Not neatly, but it fits. It is a part of my history that I no longer deny, and like all life experiences, it has played a role in who I am today. And who I am today will do just fine . . . I am no longer a victim of intimate assault. I am a survivor of intimate assault. They feel like very different places. I was not able to get from one place to the other in my silence or in my solitude. I was not able to get there in the silence of society, for society rarely soothed me or encouraged my voice. But I cannot blame society unless I blame myself. I choose to blame neither. I simply long for the common desire to understand and undo the damage our silence and tolerance has created in our world.

It is in our silence that emotional scars are deepened and become more difficult to repair. The manner in which we are there for victims of intimate assault and abuse plays a huge role in their opportunity for recovery and their healing pace. It is imperative that victims receive attention in a timely manner in order to recover in a timely manner. Medical attention without delay is necessary to check for physical injury and address STD (sexually transmitted disease) prevention and pregnancy issues. Reporting to law enforcement and immediate forensic exams are instrumental in pursuing legal justice and often become the first step the victim takes to reclaim control of her life. Emotional support at this same time can ensure the victim will soon become the survivor.

Asking for what we need has always seemed to be a difficult request for many people to make. It is easier to assume that others know what we need as we await anxiously for them to indulge that need. And, of course, we are always disappointed when we do not receive what we expect to receive. Husbands and wives are notorious for having an amusing kind of confidence in believing their spouses must know what they are thinking and surely will act on it without anyone ever having to utter a single word. Not the best exercise for healthy communication in a marriage. And I have yet to meet a legitimate mind reader, so the chances are nil that someone, anyone, might spontaneously know and act on what we need from them.

However, it is true that most people have some kind of understanding when it comes to traumatic events such as a death, frightening crimes, serious illnesses, and traumatic accidents. Little needs to be said as we act on what is needed of us. Family and friends and even strangers are very capable of stepping up and are often there without having been asked. But this often is not the case with crimes of intimate assault and abuse.

This is not a blame game. It is just part of my rant. And it all goes back to the silence—that nasty old silence that has kept society passively ignorant and victims fearful of their own voice. It goes back to the "vicious cycle" I referred to earlier. Society cannot understand because victims do not tell. Victims do not tell because society does not understand.

I believe the emotional complexity of these crimes has made it difficult for victims to articulate the depth of their pain and the confusing emotional aftermath that can interfere in their desire to become the survivor. How do they translate their emotions into words so that others will understand what their spirit has suffered? The frustrating result will often be their silence. But this silence has never promoted healing. It has never benefited the victim/survivor. Or society. It has kept intimate assault and abuse the traumatic event that few know what to do with. Family, friends, community, society. It is time we find the words and speak out. And keep speaking out until people are listening. The understanding will begin and the ignorance will fade. And we must ask for what is needed.

I notice the thin, middle-aged man as I'm picking out bananas and broccoli in the produce section of the market. He is wearing very dark sunglasses. That has always been an interesting concept to me. Sunglasses indoors. But it is the six-inch leather knife sheath hanging from his belt that really gets my attention. I don't like knives, and this isn't a little pocket knife. But to each his own. He is just doing his thing . . . After several minutes in the produce section, I have what I need. I see Knifeman still wandering around the fruits and vegetables. He has no grocery cart, and he still has no produce in his hands. Odd. I start down the first aisle of canned goods feeling a little sense of relief at leaving Knifeman behind. But I turn and there is Knifeman slowly wandering down the same aisle and then again down the next aisle. Still no groceries in his hands. My anxiety is beginning to simmer, and I quickly tell myself to stop it. Just stop being so nervous. If I see a store employee I will calmly mention the curious man to him. Perhaps he can watch him. I am sure he is harmless, but the employee can just watch . . . I see no store employee, but I no longer see Knifeman either. He is gone. I should feel fine now. But I am not fine. My heart is pounding; I am scared. I can feel tears welling up in my frustration at the foolishness of it all. The foolishness of my emotions. Every male passing me in the aisle now looks menacing to me. The frail, little old man passing me with his cart stops my heart. The young sixteen-year-old dragging behind his mom looks so threatening. I am fearful of every man in this store. I have never felt this way. Never. Why now? Why thirty-seven years later? I think to myself this is what it feels like to go crazy. I am paralyzed, not knowing what to do. I am afraid to move. Paul has to come and get me. I have to ask him to help me. This is not like the other times when I have been able to work through my "episodes" alone. No need to bother anyone. This time I need to ask him for help . . . Paul comes as fast as he can, not wasting time on questions. He is just there.

For some reason the PTSD is back, and I am aware of my need for therapy refresher sessions. Sandra and I have decided to try EMDR (Eye Movement Desensitization and Reprocessing). It is a form of psychotherapy developed to treat trauma-related disorders. Distressing memories are reprocessed in hopes of diminishing their negative influence as better coping mechanisms are generated. I have heard of EMDR in the past but was fearful of the process. It requires the courage to look deep into that dark place and challenge it once and for all. I know it will not be easy. I trust Sandra and I have to believe I can do this. I am ready for this . . . I was right. This is not easy. But Sandra is patient and she is gently guiding me through every terrifying moment and every moment of glorious realization . . . I am drained. I have no energy left in me as I leave Sandra's office and walk to my car. I climb into my car and sit. Just sit. I give myself several minutes before I find the strength to turn the key in the ignition and begin the drive home. Every part of my body feels heavy under the weight of sadness and grief. I know I have to allow it to work its way through my whole body before I can spit it out for good . . . This feels different. I feel different. I do not want to be alone with this sadness. I am choosing to not be alone with this anymore. Reaching out for support will expose my raw emotions, I know. I will be vulnerable. But my vulnerability will also be the most honest and real me. I will ask for what I need . . . I call Jan and ask if I can stop by on my way home from my appointment. I tell her I will be there in a few minutes . . . Jan is my best friend from high school. We have been sister-friends for almost forty years. We are as different as sisters can be, but we love unconditionally, as sisters love. Over the last four decades, our life experiences and our life interests have slowly steered us in individual directions, shifting us into the differences of night and day. But these differences will never be enough to separate our hearts. I am there for her. She is there for me. And I need Jan today . . . She answers the door and immediately takes me in her arms. She knows I simply need to be with her. She knows the best thing for me right now is the comfort and safety of her embrace and the permission to sob from the very depths of my soul. I only have to tell her I do not want to be alone with this anymore. I only have to tell her I am tired of it all. I weep and she weeps with me. She holds me tight, fearing my tormented sobs will split my body in two. I cry until there are no more tears left to seep out of my body . . . We can talk about these things now. It is not like years ago when the subject of my rape was something we did not acknowledge. Today our conversations flow freely and honestly. Jan will tell me she could not imagine or begin to know what I had gone through as a result of my rape. And I am grateful she cannot know what that feels like. I do not want anyone to ever know what that experience is like. In the past it was difficult for her to know what to say or do. And so, like many of us do in that situation, we simply stay silent. We were all a product of a silent society . . . Jan will never know the reality of my pain. She was not in my shoes. She does not ever need to know that reality. What she does know and is now forever quick to act on is her gift of love, support, compassion, and hugs. She has played a most important part in the healing of my spirit, and I am filled with such gratitude for these gifts she brings to my life.

The physical, emotional, and spiritual healing of trauma is always possible, even after the most tragic of events. We have witnessed this time and time again. It is the resiliency of humanity. Conscious choices are made to move forward toward a more positive life focus. Time heals. Memories dull. Life goes on. Victims become survivors. We do this best when we are able to lift each other up, when we are able to carry another just briefly until their strength returns.

Find your support. Find it in those you trust, in those whose lives move in and out of your own. Be the support. Be there for someone when their world unravels and when all they need to know is that they are not alone.

*   *   *

I met an amazing group of women seven years ago while attending the Sexual Assault Support Service (SASS) training program to begin my work with victims of intimate assault. The classes were informative, eye-opening, and intense. Very intense. Not only did we open ourselves up to learn and absorb the disturbing reality of intimate assault, but along the way we also opened up places in ourselves we had not planned on visiting. Needless to say, this group of ten women quickly bonded.

It was obvious that our initial bond was due to our common passion to make a difference in the fight against intimate violence. We all had our individual reasons for wanting to do our small part to stop the silence, to end the social tolerance, and to bring about better awareness. Most importantly, we all wanted to be there for victims who would need unconditional support as they journeyed toward recovery.

By the end of the SASS training program, several of us were not ready to go our separate ways and take the chance of not staying connected. There were six of us who decided that meeting for ice cream after our final class was a good idea. So off we went.

Seven years later, we are still eating ice cream together and gushing over the incredible fortune we have found in each other. Ours is a friendship like no other, and not a minute goes by that we are not completely aware of how blessed we are to have each other. These friendships are uniquely unconditional. These are relationships without judgment, and they are based on a deep respect for each other and for our differences. And we are definitely different.

Erica Jones is a thirty-something, single, independent, intelligent, and vibrant prosecuting attorney. A feminist? Perhaps, but only in the very best sense of the word.

Ida Seiferd, lover of horses, has not quite left her twenties. She is a mom, wife, social worker. Ida has a serious dream as she presently studies for her masters in equine therapy. Her dream is the ranch that will someday shelter kidnapped and trafficked girls as they heal and recover their sense of self.

Dr. Mindy Hsu (I am laughing because I think very few people know Mindy has earned the title of Doctor, and I do not believe I have ever heard her use this well-deserved title herself) is also thirty-something, single, and the never-ending volunteer. She is a pharmacist and an American Mensa member (I had to throw that in there).

Nicole Schauwecker is a wife, mother, and full-time employee with our sheriff's department. Nicki beautifully represents the forty-somethings. With her plate so full it never ceases to amaze me how she piles it even fuller as she routinely volunteers herself for one important cause after another.

Sheila Barrett was our sixth beautiful woman. I say *was* because we lost Sheila far too soon. Sheila had a strength about her that few could match. So losing her fight against cancer came as a terrible blow to all who loved her. Sheila was a nurse practitioner and a SART nurse examiner who cared for others with her warm compassion and genuinely supportive nature. We miss her terribly.

These women represent a support system that I wish all could know. My hope is that at any given time, for any given reason, all could experience just one of these incredible connections to the loving care and concern each of these women so easily offers. Few of us will ever get through life without experiencing the need for compassionate support, and likewise, all of us will always have the opportunity to be the giver of that same support. This is how we collectively heal. This is how victims become survivors. This is how simply being there for each other makes us all our best self.

We call ourselves the "SASSypants." Erica, Ida, Mindy, Nicki, and I. It's a silly name but suits us well . . . I am excited for our quick overnight road trip to Ashland. We are all going to see a play Erica saw a few months ago, and she says we must all go see it together. It is an important play with an important theme. But she says we have to bring tissues. We will cry . . . We are standing in line outside the theater waiting in anticipation to see "Ruined." This play opened in New York in 2009 and eventually won a Pulitzer Prize. It takes us to Africa, to the war in the Democratic Republic of the Congo, where the brutality against females is unimaginable. The play is set deep in the jungle and from there goes even deeper into the souls of their women. I look behind me in line and see that Mindy took Erica's suggestion of tissue very seriously. She does not have a few tissues in her hand; she has brought the entire large-size box of tissue with her. We laugh at her (always with love) but later we are apologizing. Turns out we needed that whole box of tissue . . . In our hotel room we are emotionally drained from the intensity of this play. We have plenty to say, knowing the play's storyline is taken from real life conditions in the Congo and that similarities of these women's grievous oppression and inspiring courage continue to exist globally . . . I drift off to sleep with images of the actresses portraying with exact emotion the pain and darkness of life in the Congo. I am awakened by these same images in the still-dark hours of the early morning. My heart is heavy with a sadness for the pain so many must endure. I keep seeing actress Chinasa Ogbuagu's character, Salima, in my mind. I see her face and know her acting is precisely representing the soul pain of so many women. I try to hold back my tears, not wanting to wake my SASSypants scattered throughout the room sleeping soundly. But one by one, they sense me stir, and in the darkness our conversation begins. Quietly we are gathered on my big bed, speaking as only the dearest of friends can speak. I am safe with these women. They know my wounds, I know theirs. I tell them that when the pain gets too unbearable I just want to run and run and keep on running. And I want to scream it all out. As loud as I can. I want to scream out the ugliness of my pain and the pain that so many others quietly endure. I want to scream through the silence that has kept the haunting memories from fading into nothing . . . So that's it. We are going to scream. Erica, Ida, Mindy, and Nicki tell me we are going to find the perfect spot on our drive home so that I can scream. And they will scream with me . . . We are not having much luck finding just the right place for our scream. We pass forest after forest that seems ideal for a scream fest, but when we pull off the road into the trees we notice there are campers who most likely would not appreciate the piercing noise of our screams. We travel on. I am thinking to myself that it is okay if we do not find the perfect location. Maybe I do not really need to scream. I have survived this long without the scream. Is it going to make a difference? But even Sandra, my former therapist, had once encouraged me to scream out my frustration if that's what it took. And my SASSypants are not giving up. They are going to see to my scream . . . We come upon the burnt forest that we had passed the day before on our drive to Ashland. We all are thinking the same thing. Perfect! No worries about disturbing other humans or even the animals with our noise. Campers rarely hang out in the charred aftermath of a destructive fire, and the four-legged creatures quickly moved on to new homes. The ruined forest. This is where we will scream. We carefully maneuver our car off the road and as far into the burnt woods as possible. We pile out of the car and immediately connect the silence and bleakness of the darkened woods to our purpose and our need to scream. One by one we gather our own personal and separate thoughts, our reasons for wanting to rid our beings of all that weighs us down. And one by one we scream. We scream loud and deliberately. We scream out our frustrations, our negativity. We scream out the bleakness and sorrow of life that attempts to hold us back. We scream for those who have not yet screamed and for those whose pain we continue to share. We scream because we can, because we own our strength as women and honor our spirits as human beings. We are screaming through the silence of this beautiful darkened forest.

*　　*　　*

"I was raped thirty-one years ago, and there are days that I don't feel like a survivor. There are times I wake up in the middle of the night dreaming about my attack. How can I feel

like a survivor at that time? The dream mentally attacks me over and over, and when I wake up, the rape is still going on in my head. I am crying, feeling alone and hopeless and once again a victim, not feeling like a survivor . . . Through a strong support system and proper self-care, victims will no longer remain victims. They will be survivors. But no one should ever have to endure this pain alone . . . I have taken back control of my life, and with the volunteer work I do as an advocate for victims of sexual assault, I am able to be there for others when their world feels like it is crashing down on them. I now have much more power than my perpetrator will ever have."

Marissa
Intimate assault survivor

"Looking back, I wish I had confided in someone. I wish I had sought therapy. Dealing with the rape on my own was horrible. I still feel alone. I still feel unworthy of love . . . I wish this encouragement for survivors to speak out was around when I was younger. It would have been nice to know that I was not alone."

Sarah
Intimate assault survivor

"It's been over thirty years and I can finally have the freedom to be happy. My scars belong to me. I am not ashamed of them. I have the gift of not judging myself or anyone else. I have the freedom to look in the mirror and love myself and others, no matter what. I smile at the person I have become. I have character; I am a lady. I am able to love and be loved. My spirit is whole, strong, and wise. I am what my creator meant me to be."

Aly
Intimate assault survivor

"When I was around thirty-two years old, I shared with my two brothers what had happened to me as a child. My brothers, both lawyers and well-educated, discounted it and never supported me. I felt as though they didn't believe me. Still to this day I don't think they understand the profound effect the abuse had on my life. I also don't think they have any understanding of how discounted I felt when I did not receive some kind of acknowledgment from them or hear that they were sorry that I had been hurt in that way as a child. I was close to both of my brothers and always had admired them. I always looked up to my oldest brother and felt a second violation when he discounted my sexual abuse . . . It is strange what comes from bad events in one's life. On one hand, I became a stronger and better person because of it, but on the other hand, the abuse stole a part of my authentic self. Life goes on, and as I get older, my perspective has changed. My focus and attention have changed. I am putting my energy in different places. I am a person with a great deal of perseverance, and I have fought hard to have peace in my life. I now have made peace with it all, and I have peace in my life. My life isn't anything like I thought it would be, yet after everything is said and done, I have what I need. Peace. I take good care of myself. I have no desire for excitement. All the drama of my early years took care of that. The day to day simple life makes me happy . . . I have my sweet daughter Marie in my life, and she is all about unconditional love. It's all bittersweet."

Anna
Child intimate abuse survivor

"Pain in life is inevitable and different for each person. Just as the green grass and flowers come after the rain, new understanding and growth come after the pain. I have found

I am able to relate to people in a way I never thought I would . . . I've heard that many victims say living with the aftermath of an assault is harder than the assault itself, and I absolutely agree. The assault lasted only a few minutes, but the aftermath will last my lifetime. I don't know what it will be like next year, next week, or tomorrow. But at this point I can say that I am living. I am living as a survivor."

Jaime
Intimate assault survivor

"My name is Allecia. It has taken me most of my life to realize that I was and am a wonderful human being . . . I am constantly amazed that any human being would inflict this kind of cruelty and sadistic behavior on a child. I am blessed to be alive as my wounds are constantly being healed and then reopened . . . Now when I want something that I never received as a child I give it to myself, as if I am the parent. When Christmas comes around I buy myself my own Christmas gift and then on my birthday, my own birthday gift . . . There was a moment in my life as a child when I questioned whether I wanted to live or die. I decided to live—despite the scars on my body, my soul, and my spirit. So I started to enjoy the small things in life. The sunshine, ice cream, and just being. I think each moment that we have in this world is special, and I live my life accordingly. Each day can be wonderful. Like the wonderful me I am."

Allecia
Child intimate abuse survivor

"It has taken me a long time to be comfortable in my own skin and to validate this female body of mine. I've been to hell and back. The battle was long, intense, and life-threatening. My life has been no accident, and my experiences were allowed for a reason. I dug deep and relied not only on my

own understanding but on the truth of God helping me find my voice—helping me become victorious and the woman I am today."

A. G.

Intimate assault survivor, child intimate abuse survivor

"I couldn't go around them, over them, or even under them anymore. I had to finally acknowledge that the only way out of the emotional, mental, and spiritual pain was to go right through the middle. I made a decision to acknowledge all my feelings, and I have come to understand that they are there to direct me. Today my feelings let me know what is going on inside of me, and I honor and acknowledge them. I've learned that my feelings will not destroy me but instead will make me stronger. I believe that my life, my own life, is worth living. I've also come to realize that I am stronger than I ever thought I was."

Nanette
Intimate assault survivor

Afterword

Some forty years later I remain acutely aware of what was taken from me as a young and innocent eighteen-year-old girl. The clarity of this memory actually surprises me. Because forty years is an awfully long time to carry a memory. But life is not perfect, and memories do not always fade into nothingness. Today I can say I am actually grateful for this particular imperfection of life. Because it is this continued awareness and memory, this imperfection in my life, that has contributed to the sum of who I am. And today I lovingly welcome the woman I have become.

This awareness keeps me focused on the work I choose to do and will not let me forget what needs to be done for those who continue to be harmed in a most undeserving way. It does not allow me to forget those innocent spirits whose pain will seep deeper into their being if left alone in their darkness. Perhaps forgetting is not always a good thing. Perhaps today I am where I am meant to be in my life—and for today, this is enough.

This awareness is what drives me to know the importance of the sound of a voice, no matter how many other voices are silent. No matter how many other voices are talking around and over an issue.

The survivors who shared their experiences with me and contributed to this book are not celebrities. They are not well-known personalities who are used to hearing their own voice. They are simply survivors who represent thousands and thousands of other victims and survivors who need and deserve to be heard. They are courageous in speaking out when they know it is not comfortable but know it is necessary. They are honest with their deepest truths, hoping it will set them freer and freer with every word. Most importantly, these survivors are willing to speak out for the sake of others who they know are going through the same darkness they themselves once endured. All are hopeful that their voices will encourage the voice of another. There is strength in numbers, and I am tremendously grateful for the strength and courage these survivors have been so willing to share. Little by little this is how it is done.

I have been asked more than once if writing this book has been healing for me and was that my intention in writing. My answer is that I did not write this book with my healing in mind; that was not my intention. After all, I am already a survivor. I was compelled to write purely out of frustration at what I was observing over and over again in our society, at what I was hearing and not hearing. I wrote because I cannot know what I know about the pain of intimate violence and remain silent. I wrote because others continue to suffer, often in their self-imposed silence, fearing society's tolerance and lack of understanding. And this knowledge tears at my heart. I wrote for all the gifts in my life: my children, grandchildren, nieces, nephews, family, and friends. I wrote for every precious innocent face I see day in and day out. Silence for me these days is simply not an option. I wrote to rant.

But those asking me the question of the healing effect of my writing were actually far more insightful than I. Because my answer today is although my intention for writing was not with my own healing in mind, I have to say something feels different. It is a very good kind of different. It is a strength that grew even stronger. A gratitude that grew more grateful. An unexpected freedom that emerged with every word pounded out on the keyboard. It is my voice on paper.

I am validating my voice as much as I choose to validate the voice of others. And this sound has been a long time coming.

There was a time when I was not able to fight back, when I did not have it in me to fight back. I did not try to run, or scream for help, or kick and scratch my way out. And I did not tell. I was in the midst of something too horrible to grasp, too shocking and confusing to absorb. So the best I could do was fold into myself.

None of that is good enough for me today. I know my silence back then very likely allowed my rapists to confidently move on to their next victim, to destroy another spirit, anticipating the continued silence. The weight of that knowledge is heavy, and I carry it every day.

But today is a new day, and today I choose to fight back. I just have found a different way of fighting. And this fight matters to me more than ever. I fight back every time I sit beside and comfort the latest victim who feels wounded to her core. I fight back as I use my voice in conversation, hoping to bring about a better awareness and understanding to those who may care, hoping to touch those who may not. I fight back as I lend my support to others who took up this fight as their own long before me, making a positive difference in those injured lives that must always matter.

This fight must be our collective fight. Our tolerance is proportionate to our silence. Society must be encouraged to get to a place of outrage and intolerance, a place that has no room for the myths and misconceptions held tightly for so many generations. Our children deserve to grow up with their spirits intact, not fractured because we chose to look the other way in our quiet discomfort. Stopping the silence can get us there.

Last year Paul and I were vacationing in New York City. One evening as we were strolling along the streets of Manhattan, we passed an elegant jewelry shop with its front window brightly lit, illuminating all the colorful and precious gems on display. We did not stop to peek in the window (I am not a fine jewelry kind of girl, much to Paul's delight), but I happened to glance over and notice the most exquisite Faberge egg in the display case. We continued walking several steps past the shop before I felt a tug, a sense of familiarity, pulling me back to the window. "Just a minute, Paul, I want to go back and look at something." I walked toward the decorated window and looked, really looked, at the Faberge egg. It was beautiful, delicate, and fragile. And it was valuable.

Paul asked me what had caught my eye. Pointing to the lovely piece, I told him, "The egg." I explained, feeling content in the moment, "Paul, that is how I see my spirit. That is what my spirit feels like to me these days. It is precious and delicate and fragile. I picture my spirit looking just like that uniquely beautiful egg. The only difference is my Faberge egg spirit was once broken into hundreds of jagged pieces. And when I was finally able to put all those pieces back together, they didn't fit quite the same as they once did. You can barely see the cracks, but I know they are there. Still, it is whole and it is lovely. And it is so very valuable."

IF YOU HAVE BEEN THE VICTIM OF INTIMATE ASSAULT

- Tell someone. A trusted friend, family member, teacher, school counselor, or coworker. You will need the support and direction they can offer.

- Seriously consider reporting the crime to law enforcement. Not only will this give you access to medical treatment and resources that will benefit you, but it can be the first step in regaining your control that was briefly and unfairly taken from you.

- If you report, do not bathe, douche, or change your clothes. Do not disturb the crime scene area.

- Do not blame yourself. No matter what your behavior or actions were, rape is never the appropriate consequence. Only the perpetrator is to blame.

- Be patient with yourself. You have been traumatized, and your healing is a process that may take time.

- Consider professional counseling or a support group.

What You Can Do for a Loved One Who Has Survived Intimate Assault

- Be supportive, be patient, and listen. Then listen some more.
- Be sensitive with the questions you may be compelled to ask. What he/she was doing, saying, using, or wearing is not significant. He/she was the victim of a crime, not the perpetrator.
- The victim may be experiencing feelings of guilt. He/she must be reminded it was not his/her fault.
- Give your loved one time to sort through the complex emotions that may come and go. Healing can be a long process, and patience is necessary.
- Encourage the victim to report the crime to law enforcement, but respect their decision if he/she chooses not to.
- Encourage the victim to seek medical care. Medications for possible sexually transmitted disease exposure and pregnancy prevention are available.
- Encourage the victim to seek counseling.

WHAT WE CAN DO TO FIGHT INTIMATE VIOLENCE

- Recognize the myths and misconceptions regarding rape and abuse. Advocate intolerance.
- Speak out. Stop the silence and discomfort surrounding this issue. Our silence has enabled the perpetrator to move from victim to victim.
- Support your local rape/crisis center by volunteering or consider a financial donation that can assist them in their outreach programs.
- Write a letter of support to a company that is promoting positive images of women. Or write a letter of complaint to companies that promote disrespect and violence against women, children, and men.
- Encourage your child's school to provide students with age appropriate education and awareness regarding intimate assault and abuse. Also encourage schools to offer adult discussions during PTA or school board meetings.
- Protest sexism in the media. Do not support movies, television, or radio that encourage a violent culture.
- Although the majority of intimate assault victims are female, we need the help of men, as well as women, to create awareness.
- Men must be mindful of the type of role model they are to the young boys and males in their lives. Lead by example.

- Men can let other men know when they are making inappropriate or disrespectful comments of any kind against any female. Most men do not normally speak out about these issues. Do not be afraid to stand up and say the right thing.
- Talk and listen to the women in your life. Ask them how you can help.
- Men must make this issue their business. Our communities need the influence of good, strong, decent males who are willing to speak out and make a positive difference in the fight against intimate violence.

Resources

National Sexual Assault Hotline (operated by RAINN)
1-800-656-HOPE
Free. Confidential. 24/7.

RAINN (Rape and Incest National Network)
Online Hotline: www.rainn.org
Free. Confidential. 24/7.
Search for crisis centers in your area on the RAINN website
Or call 1-800-656-HOPE

Men Can Stop Rape: Creating cultures free from violence
For more information go to: www.mencanstoprape.org

Green Dot, etc.
The primary mission of Green Dot, etc. is the reduction of power-based personal violence (intimate violence, partner violence, bullying, stalking, child abuse or elder abuse) with the goal of preparing communities to implement bystander intervention strategy.
No one has to do everything . . . everyone has to do something. What's your Green Dot?
For more information go to: livethegreendot.com

Acknowledgments

I cannot remember a moment in my life when I have not felt an abundance of gratitude for the people tightly laced throughout my world. My too-numerous-to-count family members and friends continuously brought joy and love to the good part of my life, the part that did not require the "mask." But these days, the mask has been tossed aside for the most part, and I feel my gratitude overflow as our never-ending journey toward growth, understanding, and mutual support continues. To acknowledge this gratitude, I must start at the beginning, *my* beginning. Ten years ago.

I will never know the name that belonged to the voice on the other end of the phone as I dialed that number searching for help so long ago. I will never be able to wrap my arms around her voice in a warm embrace and say, "Thank you, you changed my life." But I can say "thank you" to the countless volunteers who generously give of themselves day after day simply to be there for others during their darkest moments. You do make a difference.

Thank you, Misty Allen, for reintroducing me to my power and my courage. Your voice gently led me to my voice.

Kim Garrett, Caitlyn Wallace, Alma Razo, and Pam Young. You four women will forever hold a uniquely special place in my heart. You provided knowledge and a trusted shelter, allowing me to safely explore my worth.

Your passion to create a better world inspires me to do the same. I love you and thank you.

Ben Felix, my fearless leader with a heart of gold. Thank you, dear man, for fighting the good fight and for being my constant support. I love you. Muah!

Sally Walker, Janett Massolo, Cassondra Schoppe, Debbie Gant-Reed, Kathy Jacobs, Tina Schweizer, and Kasey Lafoon. My "muscles" stay strong because of women like you. Thank you for your dedicated and tireless work.

I am so grateful for your encouragement, Shelly Reynolds, nudging me to keep plugging along, putting my thoughts on paper. When my doubts began creeping about, you reminded me I will have succeeded if just one person reads my words and is touched. Because that one person matters. Much love and gratitude to you.

Thank you, Sandra Poupeney, for providing a most kind and professional sanctuary that, I must say, didn't always feel so warm and fuzzy. But warm and fuzzy was not what I needed as you guided me to that place of healing and emotional health. I am forever grateful for your patience and sincere compassion.

More than just my go-to, can-you-help-me-with-this, let's-go-eat friend, Dori Mendiola, you are my easy, comfy pal who never fails to brighten my day. Thank you for your support and encouragement. I love you, dear friend.

Jan Federici, sister-friend and my heart's twin. Our precious friendship has endured more than forty years, and our personal growth is worth celebrating. The journey continues, and I am so grateful you are by my side. I love you.

Marissa, Sarah, Tina, Dee, Aly, Anna, Amy, Allecia, Jaime, A. G., Nanette, Ida, and Cita. To pair words with your pain and speak your truth is courageous and necessary. Thank you for trusting me with your voices. Deep peace to you all.

Denyse McElroy, you were wise beyond your years, and when my thoughts take me "back in the day," it is your face I still see. No one could hold a light to that place you held in my heart. I am eternally grateful for all we share, yesterday and today. I love you always, my forever sister.

Brandon Williamson, you "get it," and that puts a smile on my face. Thank you for understanding this issue also belongs to you.

A girl can't have too many brothers, and I am one of the lucky ones. Fred McElroy, Howard McElroy, Georgie McElroy, Paul McElroy, and Tommy McElroy. My life is indeed richer with the blessings of love (and laughter) that tie our family together. You are my safe havens. I love you all.

Jane Miller, Carol Salika, and Theresa Simko. You are more than just my sisters and more than just my friends, and I am forever grateful for sharing my life with you. We have gotten to that place where silence is not allowed, and it is a very good place to be. Thank you for your loving support and for those conversations where you found yourselves listening more than you were speaking. Thank you for understanding my desire to write and for your gentle critiquing of my work. I love you all dearly.

I'm not sure if I will even bother searching for the right words to describe that place in my heart that embraces my *SASSypants*: Ida Seiferd, Mindy Hsu, Erica Jones, and Nicki Schauwecker. Because sometimes words simply are not sufficient. This may be one of those times. But I will tell you, sisters of my soul, what you already know: that you all are my treasured friends whose honesty, unconditional love, and unwavering support constantly raise me up and encourage me to be my best self. I can't imagine a day without your beautiful spirits. I love you all.

Angela and Natalie, you are the very best and most precious gifts that have blessed my life. I am so grateful for the lessons that daughters teach mothers. I love you to the moon and beyond—and then beyond even that.

And lastly, the keeper of my heart. Thank you, Paul, for never giving up on me, for never making me feel it was all just too much. I have no doubt where you are these days. You are here, simply here. For me. I love you.

Works Cited

Gray, John. *Men Are from Mars, Women Are from Venus.* New York: HarperCollins, 1992.

Groth, Nicholas A., and Birnbaum, H. J. *Men Who Rape: The Psychology of the Offender.* New York: Plenum Press, 1979.

Katz, Jackson. *The Macho Paradox: Why Some Men Hurt Women and How All Men Can Help.* Naperville: Sourcebooks, 2006.

Katz, Jackson. *Tough Guise: Violence, Media and the Crisis in Masculinity*, DVD. 82 minutes. Directed by Sut Jhally. Northampton: Media Education Foundation, 1999.

Made in the USA
San Bernardino, CA
14 March 2013